ask
THE
bugman

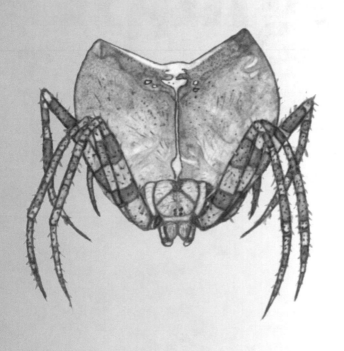

ask
THE
bugman

ENVIRONMENTALLY SAFE WAYS TO
CONTROL HOUSEHOLD PESTS

RICHARD FAGERLUND, B.C.E.,
AND JOHNNA LACHNIT

ILLUSTRATIONS BY
JOHNNA LACHNIT

UNIVERSITY OF NEW MEXICO PRESS
ALBUQUERQUE

Library of Congress Cataloging-in-Publication Data

Fagerlund, Richard, 1943–
     Ask the bugman : environmentally safe ways to control household
pests / Richard Fagerlund and Johnna Lachnit ; illustrations by Johnna
Lachnit. — 1st ed.
        p.   cm.
A compilation of questions and answers which appeared in the author's
column, Ask the bugman in the Albuquerque tribune from March 1997
to March 2000 and now in the San Francisco chronicle.
ISBN 0-8263-2835-0   (pbk. : alk. paper)
     1. Pests—Integrated control—Miscellanea.   2. Insect pests—Integrated
control—Miscellanea.   I. Lachnit, Johnna, 1973–   II. Title.
     SB951 .F25 2002
     648'.7—dc21

                                             2001006998

Contents

Foreword

Insects have been the dominant animals on earth for millions of years. Their activities are studied constantly because they interact with almost every aspect of life. Unfortunately, humans have developed an attitude toward insects of disgust, loathing, and paranoia, which is a very unfair view because humans are taught little about the wonders of this micro-world. Long ago, the saying "the only good bug is a dead bug" was taken to heart by the populace and was acted upon by young and old alike, taking the killing of any bug as an act that would save the world.

This book is an attempt to help humans look at insects in a different light—not as total adversaries, but as animals that are not vicious or nasty but worthy of life too. Dick Fagerlund approaches management as a way to keep homes for humans safe and enjoyable, using common-sense approaches when dealing with our microscopic earthly companions, including insects and spiders and even some bigger animals such as snakes, rodents, and the like. Dick has engaged his friend and coauthor Johnna Lachnit in discussions about topics involving pesticide use and hemp, to add another voice of reason on controversial subjects.

Encounters with insects around homes do not require all-out war, using chemicals as an army uses armaments. Rather, one needs an understanding of how the bug acts, where it typically lives, and what it needs for survival, and then discovering what the people are providing in these areas so that they can change to make their homes less attractive. People have always asked questions, and Dick has taken this opportunity to use newspapers as a forum, to hear the questions, and provide sound, logical courses of action that allow people to really solve problems, not just mask them as so often has been the case with the overuse of pesticides so common to our society today. He has taken his weekly newspaper columns, organized them to provide many scenarios about different insects viewed as problems to homeowners around the entire United States, and then provides information about the insects and plans of action to solve the problems.

In this book, readers will learn about the lives of insects and how to understand why they interact with people and how to mediate that interaction in a much more rational way than is typically approached in the United States. It is not necessary to kill all bugs for people to enjoy their homes; in fact, the bugs might just help make the outdoors much more enjoyable. It is the hope of Dick and Johnna that humans will learn to share their space with nature, but still maintain their homes for comfortable living without major intrusions that create unhappiness.

Carl Olson, Associate Curator
Department of Entomology
University of Arizona, Tucson, Arizona

Acknowledgments

I want to thank all of the readers of my columns who contributed most of the material in this book. I also want to thank Kevin Hellyer *(Albuquerque Tribune)*, Lynette Evans *(San Francisco Chronicle)*, and Walt Veazy (Scripps-Howard News Service) for running my columns. The column runs in far too many papers to list them all here, but I want to thank all of the editors of all of the papers where it is run, either regularly or sporadically.

I also wish to thank the people I work with at the University of New Mexico who have encouraged me throughout the entire project, especially Mary Vosevich, director of the Physical Plant Department, and Gary Smith, associate director of Environmental Services in the Physical Plant Department. Mary and Gary have always been supportive of all of the bug projects I have taken on.

I am grateful to Carl Olson, University of Arizona, for reviewing the book and for writing the foreword, and to Cam Lay, Clemson University, for reviewing the book.

Next, I wish to thank the following people who have contributed to the book: Cam Lay (Clemson University); Ana Davidson (University of New Mexico); Dr. Ann McCampbell (Multiple Chemical Sensitivity Task Force of New Mexico); Paula Moore (People for the Ethical Treatment of Animals); Katy Maddox; Barbara Witterick; Joy Black; Joan Schmidt; Martha Boyce; R. E. Gentry; Anna Victoria Reich; Jane in Richmond; Sally Goodfellow; and Elliot, Emmelisa, Brittany K., Brittany H., Britney B., Tate, Lindsy, Cassidy, Jordan, Christina, Drew, Bryce, Alex, Laurel, Ryan, Manda, Mark, and Laura from Hubert Humphrey Elementary School in Albuquerque. I also want to thank my late wife Sandi for providing all of the interesting snake stories.

Last but not least, I want to thank Johnna for helping me with this project as coauthor and illustrator and in several other projects we are involved in. She is a good friend, business partner, and a major spiritual influence in my life.

Richard Fagerlund

First, I want to thank Richard Fagerlund for providing me with the opportunity to work on this book. There are many people I would like to acknowledge in the making of this book: my husband Doug and my best friend Melanie Sanchez for their support and kindness in every area of my life; Lynn Panco, who encouraged creativity in me and many others; my aunt Peggy Travis, a naturalist whose wonderful illustrative artwork has taught me about the necessity of patience in learning technique as well as the subject of my drawings, as well as respect for Mother Earth and all her progeny; my father, who through his lifelong organic gardening, kept me in touch with good food and insects; my Mom, for teaching me about color; my sister, Candice Jones, for her impact on me regarding animals and the Earth; Rita Olson, for her support; Dylan Olson, for his love and friendship through all my trials; and Jenny Olson, for helping me maintain peace of mind.

I would like to thank the many people who have helped me throughout my life to be on the path that I am today. I wish to thank the Jemez mountains, all the insects, and the New Mexico sunsets, all of which have given me the motivation to work on this book.

I am grateful to Julia Butterfly Hill for her inspiration and for showing me and others that we can make a difference, albeit by investing a lot of effort and time. I wish to thank the redwoods for the lessons they have taught Julia and me, among many others. We are blessed with their ancient presence and energy. I also thank the trees for the paper this book is printed on. Most of all, I want to thank the readers of this book; it is my hope that all of us can work together to make the world a better place by using fewer chemicals. The Divine has blessed us with all we need. Let's not alter the planet, but instead live in its beauty in the most selfless way we can.

Blessed Be to All and Especially the Trees,
Johnna "Chloe" Lachnit

Introduction

I started writing the "Ask the Bugman" column for the *Albuquerque Tribune* in March 1997. In March 2000, Scripps-Howard News Service started distributing the column to its newspapers across the United States and Canada. In August 2000, the column was picked up by the *San Francisco Chronicle*.

This book is a compilation of some of the many questions I have received as author of "Ask the Bugman." Most of the questions are of general interest and reflect the public's desire to control pests with a minimal use of pesticides. Some questions are purely entomological and others are about pesticides and the pest control industry. The book covers a wide variety of topics including, but not limited to, the principles of integrated pest management (IPM), nontoxic pest control methods, homemade baits and lures, multiple chemical sensitivity (MCS), how to hire an exterminator, homemade remedies from column readers, and readers' least favorite bugs. Most of the book consists of questions and answers as they appeared in the newspaper column, along with the reader's place of residence. Letters, emails, and comments from readers appear in boldface type, while my comments are in regular type.

I started in the pest control business in Florida in 1969. Over the next nine years I worked for different pest control companies in Florida, New York, Virginia, and Texas, before finally moving to New Mexico in December 1978. While in the business I was a route technician, salesman, service manager, sales manager, branch manager, and business owner. In 1996, I got out of the commercial pest control industry and joined the staff at the University of New Mexico where I helped develop the IPM program now in effect. I currently work for

Environmental Services in the Physical Plant Department at the University of New Mexico.

When I started in the bug business, it was quite a bit different than it is now. We used all sorts of pesticides that we wouldn't dream of using now. I drove a Chevy Malibu as a service vehicle and the trunk of the car was well stocked with DDT, chlordane, heptachlor, phosphorus paste, arsenic, cyanide, strychnine, zinc phosphide, toxaphene, and other insidious products designed to indiscriminately kill all kinds of organisms. Over the years many of those products disappeared (thank God!), and the industry moved toward more environmentally friendly methods of pest control, namely IPM. Unfortunately, some of the pest control companies are still stuck in the dark ages of pest control and use methods that are no longer acceptable, or at least, shouldn't be. The good news is that a number of the pest control companies are now practicing IPM and they are on the right track as we go into the twenty-first century. The "spray-and-pray" crowd (spray chemicals and pray it kills something) will have to be dragged kicking and screaming into the new era and many of them will go by the wayside, which is probably better for the public, the environment, and the rest of us.

I met Johnna Lachnit when she was working for the New Mexico Public Interest Research Group (NMPIRG). We developed a friendship as we had a lot in common, including our love for the environment. Johnna is a gifted artist and I asked her to illustrate this book and also to contribute some of her thoughts on a couple of subjects about which she is passionate.

One of the most common questions I get is how to prevent pests from getting into a home or business. Most insects and other arthropods can be prevented from entering our homes by following a few simple suggestions. Some insecticides may be used judiciously if the homeowner doesn't object to them, but they aren't necessary. If insecticides are used, they should be restricted to cracks, crevices, and voids around plumbing. They should never be "broadcast sprayed" all around the outside of the house as this will create a dead zone and kill more beneficial organisms than pests. If you don't want to use chemicals, then you can follow these suggestions to keep your house bug free:

- Keep ground litter, firewood, loose boards, and rocks away from the foundation. They provide hiding places for scorpions, centipedes, ants, cockroaches, and other potential pests.
- Keep trees and bushes trimmed back so the branches aren't touching your house. Branches offer ants and other insects a pathway to your home.
- Don't use outside lights any more than you have to as lights attract insects and organisms that eat insects.
- Refrain from using bark mulch around the home. This material is very attractive to insects and spiders.
- Remove stumps and dead wood from your yard. This material is attractive to termites.
- Fill any cracks or crevices in the foundation with a suitable material to prevent access by ants and other small insects.
- Inspect cut wildflowers carefully before bringing them in the house. Adult carpet beetles are often found on flowers.
- Make sure all windows and doors are tight fitting and all screens are in good repair.
- Keep drain covers on all drains at night to prevent entry of cockroaches.
- Put a capful of bleach down every drain several times a week. The fumes from the bleach will discourage roaches.
- Knock down any spider webs with a broom if you don't want them around the house. Spiders will not build a web in a place where it is constantly being destroyed. There is no need to kill spiders as they feed on insects.
- Daddy longlegs can be swept from the eaves where they congregate. They are not venomous and pose no danger to anyone and should be left alone if possible.

- Paper wasps start constructing their nests early in the spring. Usually one or two wasps are present. They can be knocked down with a stream of water from a hose. They will move on to another location.

Following these simple suggestions will help ensure a bug-free home. However, no matter what precautions you take and no matter how diligent you are, an occasional insect or other arthropod will find its way in. Almost any pest can be vacuumed up and disposed of. You can place some diatomaceous earth in the vacuum cleaner bag to kill the captives.

When a bug does get into your home, how do you decide whether it is a pest that needs to be killed, or an innocent interloper that should just be put outside? There are several criteria that can be used to define a pest. Speaking for myself only, I place insects into one of two categories: pest or non-pest. The pests are then divided into three categories depending on their impact on people. I use these criteria on campus. At home, I have no pests. Any insects or arthropods in my yard or that inadvertently come into my home are guests, not pests, and if in the house, are usually just placed outside, or left alone if they do not bother me.

On campus, however, I have to be more conservative because there may be in excess of 25,000 people involved. As I said, I divide pests into three categories: disruptive, destructive, and dangerous. Pests considered dangerous (by me) are wasps and yellow jackets because their stings can seriously affect people with hypersensitivities. These pests always get immediate attention. Destructive pests damage property, such as termites, carpet beetles, insects that infest food, clothes moths, and a few others. The third category, and the one most pests fall into, is disruptive. Cockroaches that walk into a room when you have company (or during a class) are disruptive. Centipedes are very disruptive when they show up. Jerusalem crickets, sun spiders, scorpions, and vinegaroons can all be disruptive because of their appearance. In Arizona or southwest New Mexico I would consider scorpions to be dangerous, because of their ability to inflict lethal stings. But scorpions are not considered dangerous in the rest of the country.

Some pests can quickly cross the line from disruptive to damaging. A cockroach on the floor is disruptive, but if it makes its home in a box of cereal or a kitchen cabinet, then it becomes destructive. Most insects that cause damage do so in large numbers, such as termites, clothes moths, carpet beetles, certain ants, and so forth.

The reason for categorizing a pest is to help determine what needs to be done to control it, if control is necessary. Dangerous pests must be controlled even if pesticides have to be used. Pests that cause damage can be serious, but the treatment can also be serious, so a lot of thought should be given to how they are handled. Pests that are simply disruptive really do not require extreme methods of control. Typically, exclusion from the building or the placement of a pest-specific bait will work.

When pests have to be eliminated, the proper procedure would be to adopt an IPM program. You can either do this yourself or hire an exterminator who practices IPM.

Integrated Pest Management

IPM is a strategy for controlling insects, rodents, and other pests, which can be applied indoors and outdoors and in urban and agricultural settings. The overall objective in a good IPM program is to provide pest-free living and working conditions using the most economical, efficient, and environmentally safe methods of control. This objective can be achieved by developing a pest management plan suited to a building design and function. IPM utilizes regular monitoring to determine if pests are present in above-acceptable levels and, if so, determining the best method of control with a minimal use of pesticides, particularly liquid and aerosol formulations. Typical methods of control include habitat modification, improved sanitation, and the use of less-toxic, pest-specific baits.

How Does IPM Work?

IPM consists of five basic steps or principles: inspection, identification, habitat modification, mechanical control, and pesticide control.

The first step is a complete inspection of the facility to determine if any pests are present, and, if so, what existing conditions are conducive to their presence. The exterior of the building should also be inspected to locate possible points of entry for the pests. If a potential pest is found, a positive identification is essential for successful installation of an IPM program. Different species of pests have different feeding habits, reproductive cycles, preferred habitats, and other living requirements. Familiarity with the pest's biology and natural history is imperative so that proper control methods are used.

The third factor, habitat modification, includes proper maintenance of plumbing to prevent leaks (water source), repairing screens, proper food storage, and proper waste and trash disposal. Mechanical control includes the use of sticky traps, pheromone traps, and vacuums to control certain pests. Chemical control should be limited to baits if at all possible. Liquid and aerosol pesticides should never be used in buildings unless there are extreme circumstances that require their use.

How Does Traditional Pest Control Differ from IPM?

Traditional pest control depends mostly on wholesale spraying of pesticides in the hope that pests will eventually encounter the chemicals and die. Generally this treatment consists of spraying chemicals along baseboards, and is known as the "spray-and-pray" method—the applicator sprays pesticides and prays it kills something. There is no scientific basis for this kind of treatment. Pesticides sprayed haphazardly like this stay in the air for long periods of time and can have a deleterious effect on building occupants.

How Can We Tell If Our Building Is Employing IPM or the Spray-and-Pray Method?

There are several ways to tell the difference. You won't see anyone walking around with a sprayer during work hours if an IPM program is in effect. You won't smell any obnoxious chemicals that will make you want to leave the building. It is worth noting that some pest control companies advertise that they use odorless chemicals. That does not mean the chemicals are harmless; it just means that you don't know if they are affecting you or not. Keep in mind that nerve gas is odorless. Also, you will see fewer pests with an IPM program, as it is far more efficient.

If Pesticides Are Used, Would We Be Notified in Advance?

In any pest control program, whether IPM or traditional, the applicator should notify all personnel in the facility prior to any pesticide application. This is mandatory in many states.

One of the most important aspects of any IPM program is education. It is very important that everyone involved or affected know exactly what is going on at all times. They have to feel confident their pest problems will be addressed quickly and safely.

If I Need to Hire an Exterminator, What Criteria Should I Look For?

Here are some important tips you can follow when hiring an exterminator:

- Do you absolutely need an exterminator? Before you hire someone to apply pesticides in your home, make sure you have a pest problem that you can't take care of yourself. Most pests, including ants and roaches, can be easily controlled by the homeowner without going to the expense of hiring a pest control operator. The only pests that require the use of pesticides are termites, severe cockroach infestations, ticks, and a few others.
- Get three or more bids, no matter how big or small the job. There are several reasons besides cost for obtaining several bids. You want to make sure the pest control company you hire is knowledgeable about your pest problem. You will want a company that uses a minimal amount of pesticides, if any at all. You also want to compare guarantees. The more bids you get, the better your chances of determining competence.
- Do they require a monthly contract or agreement? You should never sign a contract for a monthly service where the company comes to your home to

spray your baseboards unless that is what you prefer. There are no pests so insidious that you need repeated applications of pesticides to maintain control. Any competent pest control company can eliminate a pest with a single service, and perhaps a follow-up visit. If you want to hire someone to come to your home and inspect it for signs of pests or conditions conducive to a pest problem, that is valid, but you can probably determine yourself whether you have any pests.

- *Salespeople and telemarketers.* Never accept a price over the phone. Would you let your mechanic give you an estimate without raising the hood of your car? Would you expect a doctor to quote you a price without a physical examination to determine what is wrong with you? Why would you let someone apply pesticides to your home without doing an initial inspection to determine what kind of treatment, if any, is necessary to solve your problem? How can you expect anyone to give you a fair price without seeing your home? If a door-to-door salesperson comes to your house, ask a lot of questions. Make sure the person is knowledgeable about the subject. Never sign a contract with a door-to-door salesperson without thinking for a few days about whether you need the service.

- *License and insurance.* Ask a company representative for a copy of the company's license and an insurance certificate. All states have some sort of licensing program for pest control companies. Find out who regulates the industry in your state so that you can check and see what kind of license is required. Never ever let anyone apply pesticides to your home if the pest control operator's company is not duly licensed and insured.

- *"Safe insecticides."* There is no such thing as a safe insecticide. The term is an oxymoron. Insecticides may be applied safely, but they are not safe. The suffix "cide" means death, such as in homicide, suicide, and genocide. Any company that advertises that it uses safe insecticides is misrepresenting the facts. Stay away from such companies.

- *Labels, Material Safety Data Sheets, service tickets.* Ask for copies of labels and Material Safety Data Sheets (MSDS) for any pesticides a company plans to use in your home or business. If they do not have them or do not want to furnish them, call someone else. Ask to see a copy of the service ticket they will use and ask what information will be on it. The service ticket should show the target pest, the name of any pesticide used, how much is used, where it is applied, when it was applied, and the pesticide's Environmental Protection Agency registration number.

- *Ask for references.* Any pest control company that is proud of its service will happily furnish you with references. Call some of the references, particularly those who had a problem similar to yours. Check with the Better Business Bureau to make sure the company doesn't have any unresolved problems.

There are many good pest control companies that practice IPM. There are many others that spray baseboards on a regular schedule whether you need it or not, and usually you don't need it. Use the same care in hiring an exterminator that you would use in choosing a mechanic or a doctor, and you shouldn't have any problems.

I wholeheartedly recommend several products and companies. I refer to Niban Bait for cockroach, cricket, and silverfish control in this book as well as Advance Dual Choice for ant control and Advance Carpenter Ant Bait for carpenter ant control. Some of these products are not available in stores but they can be purchased online at *http:www.callbugaside.com* or by calling 1-866-520-5050. This is the website and phone number for Bug-Aside, located in Alameda, New Mexico.

Finally, one reviewer said I showed too much empathy toward some of the bugs in this book. In that I plead guilty, but I had to reject the suggestion that I change it because some readers may not understand my empathizing with insects. I do not enjoy killing anything and that may seem like a strange statement coming from someone who has spent most of his life in the pest control business. But the fact is that I will use every means available to control pests without killing them or spraying noxious pesticides in the environment, if at all possible. Of course, I have killed a great many bugs over the years, but killing bugs has never given me pleasure. On the other hand, you have to protect life and property from insects and that occasionally means killing them. I never took this business lightly and still don't. When I was teaching entomology at the University of New Mexico, I hesitated to make my class collect insects because I thought they could learn the subject without killing anything. I try to respect all living things.

> Bugs, bugs everywhere.
> Oh my goodness, I declare!
> Creepy crawly nasty things.
> What diseases will they bring?
>
> Love those bugs environmentalists say.
> Sorry. No way! Not today.
> Oh my, never fear!
> Call the pestman quickly come here.
>
> Baseboard spraying, toxic fumes.
> My poor cat might be doomed.
> What about my baby crawling on the floor?
> Will the residue last if I open the door?
>
> The door is open, I can finally breathe.
> What is this? More bugs beneath my feet?
> Poisons, toxic fumes or my buggy blues.
> Oh my, what ever shall I do?
>
> Bugs in my house.
> Bugs in my garden.
> Oh what now? A mouse?
> Shoo you thing, what diseases you bring.

Love Mother Earth you say?
Stop spawning bugs! Please, I pray!
What benefit is this, these pests everywhere?
Does anyone have any knowledge to share?

I could love Mother Earth and love those bugs,
If I could keep them out of my rugs.
Is there a compromise we can make?
Or is compromise a silly mistake?

Help me, someone, from toxic doom.
Help me get rid of these buggy blues.
Bugs, bugs everywhere.
Help me before I tear my hair!

Johnna Lachnit

1

Disruptive Pests

🐞 Disruptive bugs are considered a nuisance by their mere presence. For instance, a cockroach running across the living room floor when you are having a party is a nuisance and will probably be disruptive. Ants are generally a nuisance, but rarely cause any damage. Most of the bugs in this section will get your attention but will do little, if any, harm. Some of these bugs will occasionally cross the line from disruptive to destructive, but for the most part they are in the former category. Cockroaches, for instance, are disruptive if they act as described above, but if they contaminate food products, they cross the line to destructive. This list is not based on any scientific criteria, and thus is entirely arbitrary.

Ants

Q *I writing to ask for your help in dealing with some ant piles at my home. I have several red ant piles in my yard that I want to get rid of. I also have a black sugar ant problem—they are entering my home through a bedroom window and sometimes the kitchen door. I have grandchildren who play in the yard and so do not want to use chemicals if I can avoid them. I remember an article you wrote in the spring about using alternatives to chemicals to control pests. I saved it somewhere and now I cannot locate it (I am sure it will show up this winter). Could you please give me some information on how to get rid of these*

ants and also how to get rid of roaches and crickets, which I occa-
sionally see in my home also?

From a reader in Albuquerque, NM

A You can eliminate ant piles in your yard by pouring hot, soapy water down the entrance hole to the mounds using a small funnel. The soap and water will penetrate most of the nest and kill the ants it comes in contact with. The ants that are coming in the house can also be sprayed with soap and water. If they persist, you should use a product called Advance Dual Choice, which works for most species of ants. Niban Bait, which is made from boric acid, works very well for cockroaches, crickets, and silverfish. Make sure you place the Niban under sinks, around hot water heaters and in other areas where roaches, crickets, and silverfish are seen. Do not place it where children or pets can come in contact with it. Always read the label when using any pesticide and make sure you completely understand the directions.

Q *Help! Our home has been infested with pharaoh ants for the last*
eight years. The problem always escalates in the summer (some
worse than others). Although they have been a nuisance through-
out the house, they are concentrated in my kitchen. They have
ruined many sealed/unsealed food items, as well as packaged
water filters!!!

I have had professional exterminators two times with only
temporary control occurring from spraying chemicals of floor/wall
areas (I was only guaranteed control). We've lived with these pests
too long. Is there any way to permanently rid our home of these
tiny red ants?

From a reader in Chicago, IL

A Pharaoh ants can be eliminated but it is difficult and will take time. The mistake the exterminator in Chicago made was spraying pesticides in the house. Pharaoh ant colonies will often split up when they encounter pesticides and ultimately get worse. It is a shame the exterminator did not know a lit-tle more about their habits, as he should have been able to eradicate them.

Using baits can eliminate these ants. A good bait mix

would be 2 parts peanut butter with 3 parts honey mixed with 1 teaspoon of boric acid per 6 ounces of mixture. This bait should be placed in short pieces of plastic straws and set on the kitchen counters and other places around the home where the ants forage. They can be taped under shelves and under cabinets. Take the electrical outlets and switch plates off the wall and tape or glue a piece of straw with bait to the inside of the plate and reattach it.

Liquid and aerosol pesticides should never be used for pharaoh ant control as they will almost always exacerbate the problem rather than solve it.

If you don't want to mix your own bait, you can buy bait specifically designed for pharaoh ants.

It may take several months for you to get control using the methods I outlined above, but it won't take eight to ten years!

Q *I have tried using ant baits from stores with no luck and I don't want to use an exterminator. Are there any homemade ant baits that work?*

From a reader in San Francisco, CA

A Yes. One good bait is made from technical boric acid. Do not use medicinal boric acid, as it is white and easily confused with sugar or salt. Mix 3 cups of water with 1 cup of sugar and 4 teaspoons of technical boric acid formulated for pest control. Wrap three or four jam jars with masking tape. For a large infestation, pour a half-cup or so of bait into each of the jars, which have been loosely packed with absorbent cotton. If you have children or pets, screw the lids tightly onto the jars and seal with adhesive tape. Then pierce the lids, making two or three small holes, and smear the outside of the jars with some of the baited syrup. Place the jars where the ants are foraging and where kids and pets can't disturb them. It may take a few days but eventually the ants will be swarming to the jars. Some of the ants will die near the jars but most will carry the poison back to the colony. Don't kill the ants massed around the jars. Just let the bait work and you shouldn't have any problem.

Q *We are near water and on termite-infested soil. However, we are not infested with them because we are treated annually. My question is related to ants and I believe they are classified as "aro-batic" ants. Do they also live in the ground? Why do we see them mostly on the walls and ceiling? They do not seem to be food hunt-ing. We have ant traps and have used bombs and sprays as well as dusting around outside doors and the house. Any other sugges-tions would be appreciated.*

From a reader in Los Lunas, NM

A Acrobat ants prefer sweet foods and are often found in areas where aphids are present, feeding on the honeydew secre-tions of these insects. They will protect aphids from preda-tors and some species will even build adobe-like shelters for the aphids to protect them from the sun. If you see them moving into the house in single file they may be searching for a nesting area. Try using Advance Dual Choice ant bait, or if you prefer, you can make your own ant bait mixing 2 parts peanut butter with 3 parts of honey and adding 1 tea-spoon of boric acid per 6 ounces of bait. Place this material where the ants will find it.

Q *I never remember how disconcerting this is until it's too late! Every spring our kitchen is invaded by hundreds and hundreds of ants. There are always at least three to four different varieties at the same time—small, large, flying, you name it. This generally lasts for 1 to 2 weeks, and they make their mass appearance early every morning. There is never any evidence of anthills outside, so I am assuming they must be living under the flagstone patio, which is outside the kitchen. Any suggestions on how to avoid this problem next spring?*

From a reader in Corpus Christi, TX

A You probably have a single species of ant. It sounds like big-headed ants, but I can't be certain without seeing them. Big-headed ants are dimorphic, which means the ants in the colony are two different sizes. The smaller ones or minor work-ers are more numerous. They gather food, usually seeds, and bring them back to the colony where the larger ants, or major workers, break the seeds open with their large head and jaws. Big-headed ants are commonly found in homes in the winter and may spend the season under the slab of the home. They will enter the home through expansion joints or where pipes penetrate the slab, much like termites. In the spring, reproductives (winged ants) appear and will try to swarm and eventually mate and start a new colony. Big-headed ants in the home usually prefer cakes, breads, and pet foods, although like most ants they will eat sweets occasionally.

I would recommend two things. First, you can place a protein bait near where you usually see them and this may stop them before they become established. Second, you can spray the ants daily as you see them with a soap and water mixture. A capful of dish soap in a spray bottle filled with water is sufficient to kill many insects, including ants.

Q *What can you tell me about carpenter ants? I have them in my yard. I am not interested in killing them; I just want to know a little about them.*

From a reader in Albuquerque, NM

A I am glad you aren't killing them just because they are there. There are many different species of carpenter ants around the world and we have at least nine species in New Mexico. The species that is common in Albuquerque is the red and black form known as *Camponotus vicinus*. Colonies of this species have been found consisting of over 100,000 workers. This is an extreme number but clearly indicates the potential of these ants. A colony that large may have as many as 40 queens, a condition known as polygyny. Most other species of carpenter ants are monogynous (possessing a single queen) and, as a consequence, are considerably smaller. Large colonies of carpenter ants often split up to form satellite colonies, a fact that is important to know if you are trying to control them. Carpenter ants are normally nocturnal and find their way around by following pheromone trails put in place by scouts. Pheromones are chemicals insects use to find food, shelter, warn of predators, find members of the opposite sex, and other functions, many of which are unknown. It is also known that carpenter ants can find their way around by using landmarks such as trees, shrubs, and the moon. Carpenter ants feed on a variety of other insects and also collect the honeydew secretion of aphids. Carpenter ants are valuable ecologically and can be an indicator species of the health of a forest. For instance, pileated woodpeckers are rarely or never seen in forests without carpenter ants. The woodpecker will not survive the winter without access to carpenter ants, which form the bulk of its winter diet. Carpenter ants also play a key role as a natural biocontrol agent of such local forest pests as tent caterpillars and spruce budworms. While some species of carpenter ants are serious wood-destroying pests in other parts of the country, our local species is only rarely a pest in wood. For instance, in the state of Washington, over 50,000 homes are treated each year by exterminators for carpenter ants and many more are treated by homeowners. In New Mexico, the problem is so negligible that no one I am aware of even keeps records of homes that are structurally damaged by carpenter ants. Usually carpenter ants in a home are simply a nuisance by their presence and they don't do any damage at all.

In other parts of the country, the dominant carpenter ants found in homes are *Camponotus modoc* and *Camponotus pennsylvanicus,* two large black ants, and they are not so easily controlled as the species found in the Southwest. These two species can cause considerable structural damage and may require the services of a professional pest management operator. Make sure you hire someone who has extensive experience with carpenter ants. Ask for and check references.

Q *I have swarming ants coming through my floor vents. How can I control them?*

From a reader in Santa Fe, NM

A Ants, like other social insects such as bees and termites, swarm to start new colonies when the existing colony gets too large to sustain itself. The winged forms, known as winged reproductives, are mostly males. The winged females give off pheromones to attract the males, which is why you generally see a lot of flying ants in one place. Different species swarm at different times of the year.

Swarmers are difficult to control because they don't eat baits. Pesticides are unnecessary, as the males, which constitute the major part of a swarm, do not live very long and the swarming activity will cease almost as quickly as it began. The best way to handle swarming ants in a house is to vacuum them up. Put some diatomaceous earth in the vacuum cleaner bag to kill the ants you suck up, or if you don't mind the smell, mothballs will work. Spraying them with soap and water can kill small swarms of a few ants.

Q *I read your column in the Home & Garden section of the* Atlantic Journal Constitution, *May 18, 2000, concerning ants. I am having difficulty with Argentine ants. I tried Combat house ant traps but they did not help. I finally gave in and called the exterminator. He sprayed the perimeter of the house (I don't spray in the house) and for a few days all was well. Then they came back not only on land but in the air (flying ants). I called the exterminator back and again he sprayed the perimeter of the house. I then purchased Combat Outdoor ant traps and placed them around the house. I also trimmed shrubs around the house. So far it's okay. (I do see them in the yard but that doesn't bother me—keeping them out of the house and my cat's bowl is my aim.) The exterminator led me to believe there was no way to be rid of the ants other than to keep on spraying at intervals. I take it from your response to the letter about ants that that is not the only thing to do. My question: What do I do to correct this situation—type of trap, bait, etc.? Thank you.*

From a reader in Atlanta, GA

A I would recommend an ant bait station called Advance Dual Choice, which works very well for most species of ants. The exterminator is misleading you in an attempt to get you to sign up for repeat services, usually on a monthly basis. Any competent pest management professional should be able to rid your home of ants in one, or at the most, two visits. Spraying the perimeter of the house is useless in my opinion for controlling ants except for the short term. They are best controlled using proper baits.

Q *As you probably know, we here in South Florida have many little critters to contend with. We keep most of them under control by using a little common sense. But, these tiny little ghost ants pose a constant challenge. They are so small that you have to focus closely on them to actually see them. It's amazing how quickly these little guys can move about. How anything that small can even have legs is beyond me. They show up, not only in the kitchen, but in bathrooms, on the screened porch, and even in closets. I would really appreciate if you have any idea on how to get rid of these little pests.*

From a reader in Port St. Lucie, FL

A I lived in Florida many years ago and have met ghost ants *(Tapinoma melanocephalum)*. It is important, if at all possible, to find the colony, which can be treated with an insecticide labeled for ants. If the colony can't be found, a baiting program should be put in place. Ghost ants prefer protein baits but will take sweets. A good homemade bait consists of mixing 2 parts peanut butter with 3 parts honey and adding a teaspoon of boric acid per 6 ounces of bait. Ghost ants will also feed on honey and liver powder mixed with boric acid. The baits should be checked in a day or two to determine if the ants have been feeding and if the bait needs to be replaced. Replace the baits as needed until the ants are gone.

Q *Hello Bugman!*

I read your column every week in the S.F. Chronicle. *I love that you give suggestions that avoid the use of pesticides.*

I currently have a problem that I was hoping you could help me with. I have ants in my car. Lots and lots of them everywhere. Have you ever encountered this before? I have no food in the car. They are crawling out of the dashboard, and seem to like the spot under the ashtray. I have sprinkled some diatomaceous earth around and put out a little bait of boric acid. Any other suggestions on how to get rid of them quickly and prevent this from happening again? It is hard to drive when there are ants crawling all over the dashboard!

A Where are you parking? If you have a lot of ants where you park the car, maybe you should either park somewhere else or get rid of the ants near the car. It is unlikely that the ants are nesting in the car (but not impossible).

Try putting some homemade ant bait in the car on paper towels or pieces of paper. Mix 2 parts peanut butter, 3 parts of honey and 1 teaspoon of boric acid per 6 ounces of mix. Place this concoction in different areas throughout the car when you aren't going to use it for a day or so. If the ants are nesting in the car, the bait should eradicate them.

Cockroaches

Q *First, I would like to tell you how much I enjoy reading your column and appreciate the information you dispense. I was glad to read the letter yesterday about the cockroach problem in the flowerbeds. We have exactly the same problem. My concern is that we have box turtles loose in the yard, and I wonder if the Baygon Bait will harm them, either by coming in contact with product itself, or by eating the dead cockroaches they find. If that is the case, do you have any other suggestions?*

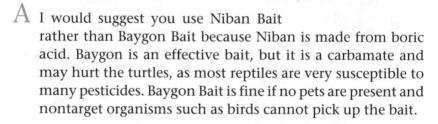

From a reader in Albuquerque, NM

A I would suggest you use Niban Bait rather than Baygon Bait because Niban is made from boric acid. Baygon is an effective bait, but it is a carbamate and may hurt the turtles, as most reptiles are very susceptible to many pesticides. Baygon Bait is fine if no pets are present and nontarget organisms such as birds cannot pick up the bait.

Q *I have small German roaches in my kitchen. I don't want anyone spraying my house. Can I get rid of them myself?*

From a reader in Chicago, IL

A Yes, but it is difficult. You have to clean the kitchen to the point where it is almost spotless. There can be no crumbs, grease, or anything else for the roaches to feed on. A roach can live for months on a single kiblet of dog food. You can place some of the commercial roach traps in your kitchen and inside your cabinets. The roaches will be attracted to the baits and they will be more effective if there are no other food sources available. Niban Bait is also very effective against most species of cockroaches.

Q *How can I keep the big, black waterbugs out of my house without using bug sprays?*
From a reader in Albuquerque, NM

A The big, black waterbugs are actually Oriental cockroaches, which are almost ubiquitous in Albuquerque. These insects frequently come up the drains at night. To prevent this you can pour a capful of household bleach down each drain several times a week and make sure the drain stoppers are in place at night. Oriental cockroaches also come in under doors, windows, and where the plumbing penetrates the wall under sinks. Doors and windows should be tight fitting and plumbing areas should be caulked or sealed. Niban Bait, which is available to the public, can be placed in areas where roaches have been seen and where pets and children cannot come in contact with it. If you use Niban Bait, make sure you read the label carefully and follow the directions explicitly. Applications of liquid pesticides are almost never necessary for controlling Oriental cockroaches.

Q *Is it possible to be allergic to cockroaches?*
From a reader in Richmond, VA

A Yes, it is possible and many people are. They are allergic to both cockroach feces and body parts. Elimination of a cockroach infestation does not necessarily eliminate the problem as the feces and body parts may still be around.

For this reason some of the better pest control companies are using specially designed vacuum cleaners to eliminate both live and dead insects and their body parts.

Q *Do cockroaches have any redeeming qualities?*
From a reader in Stuart, FL

A Everything has some redeeming qualities, cockroaches included. Cockroaches are used by researchers investigating cancer, heart disease, nutrition, and the effects of space travel. In forests, cockroaches are important in turning dead vegetation into valuable soil nutrients.

None of these important functions take place in your house, however, so you should try to control them. There are excellent baits available to the public that work very well in controlling cockroaches. Liquid insecticides are almost never necessary. Carefully read the label of any bait you use.

Q *I've read your column for quite a while, and I'm really embarrassed to ask this question so please don't use my name.*

What is so terrible about cockroaches? I am afraid friends and neighbors will think I'm pretty gross for even wondering this, but really, if you keep your foodstuffs sealed and clean your cooking surfaces, what horrible thing do they do? And is there any harm in plucking them up in your hand and tossing them outside? Either to your hand, or to lawn and garden? Catching them is almost good sport.

Along those lines, is there any reason that I should not continue my squash bug combat plan of shake the plants, squish the bugs in my fingers, and cut out sections of leaves with eggs on them? It has worked pretty well this summer, I think mainly because I started early and aborted the majority of hatches. But my friends think it's disgusting that I touch them.

In general, it's not that I get some thrill out of squishing bugs, but I'm just really hesitant to use pesticides for problems that really aren't affecting me that much, and at least with the squash bugs I've really been able to keep them in check with this simple measure. And I do wash my hands.

From a reader in Albuquerque, NM

A No, there is nothing wrong with picking up cockroaches with your bare hands. I do it quite frequently much to the dismay of anyone around me. Certainly I wash my hands after doing this as I do after touching almost anything of a foreign nature.

Cockroaches are no "dirtier" than crickets, grasshoppers, or any other bug you may encounter, although the ones that come up the drain from the sewer system may have pathogens on them, but nothing a little soap and water won't kill.

Cockroaches have a bad reputation, deserved or not, so

handling them almost always makes people squeamish. It is just a matter of perception. Not only can you handle them but they are perfectly edible, although I wouldn't recommend cooking the roaches found around town. There are roach ranchers that can furnish you with squeaky clean cockroaches if you want to cook up a batch of "Cockroach a la King." That recipe, by the way, requires 36 frozen American cockroaches. If anyone wants the recipe, they should obtain a copy of *The Eat-a-Bug Cookbook* by David George Gordon (available at *http://www.amazon.com*).

I prefer not to squish squash bugs with my fingers, however. I would prefer to step on them or hit them with something. I do applaud your reluctance to use pesticides unnecessarily.

Crickets

Q *I have crickets and I want to get rid of them without using any chemicals at all, if possible. I don't even want to use baits because they have chemicals. Is there any way to trap these critters?*

From a reader in Reno, NV

A Yes there is. You can lay some strips of duct tape, sticky side up, near where you suspect the crickets to be hiding. For some reason they are attracted to something in duct tape and they will investigate the tape and get stuck. You can then just dispose of the crickets and the tape.

Q *We moved in to a new home last summer and we are very annoyed by the crickets in the house. We think they are coming through the bathroom ventilator and probably through the screen door. How can we get rid of them?*

From a reader in Albuquerque, NM

A A good method of controlling crickets in the house is with the use of Niban Bait. This product works great on roaches and crickets. The good news is that crickets can't breed in the house, as they have to lay their eggs in soil. The bad news is that they are capable ventriloquists and they are not always where they appear to be. Put some bait under and around dressers in the bedrooms or anywhere else you suspect they are hiding. Crickets, for some reason, seem to have a fondness for chewing on personal items of apparel and are often found in dresser drawers. Try to get your screen doors to seal tightly by installing drag strips. This will help keep the crickets and other bugs out. It is not necessary to spray your baseboards with pesticides to control crickets.

Q *I read your column, "The Bugman," in the* Richmond Times-Dispatch *and find it very informative.*

My question is on camel crickets, humpback crickets, or jumping spider crickets. I have heard them referred to by all of those names but I don't know what they are really called. They are medium brown and they can really jump when you go to kill them.

Are they something new to this area, given that I had never seen one until about two years ago? Now I have lots of them and had the exterminator spray around and under the house. I still see a few in the house; they seem to like to get in the bathtub. I close the drain pipe at night but I wonder if they are coming in through the overflow pipe or maybe the furnace vents.

Do they bite, and other than being a nuisance, are they harmless? Is there something I can do to keep them away? Do the plug-in things that let out sounds that we can't hear help?

From a reader in Virginia

A Camel crickets are perfectly harmless and they do not bite. Those sonic plug-in "things" are worthless in my opinion. You can control them yourself without the help of an exterminator.

Niban Bait, which is made from boric acid, works very well for camel crickets as well as other varieties of crickets, most cockroaches, and silverfish.

Daddy Longlegs

Q *Daddy longlegs are congregating all around my eaves. Are they as deadly as I have heard and how do I get rid of them?*

From a reader in Denver, CO

A Daddy longlegs or harvestmen, as they are more correctly called, are often mistaken for spiders. Like spiders, they are arachnids, but they are not venomous at all and cannot bite people. Harvestmen feed on insects, dead animal material, and plant juices. In the fall they often congregate around the eaves of a house, in sheds, in garages, and in woodpiles. They can easily be swept from the eaves or vacuumed up. If you vacuum them, make sure you put a couple of mothballs or diatomaceous earth in the vacuum cleaner bag to kill the contents. No chemicals are necessary to control these interesting animals.

Before you write me and tell me you have been bitten by harvestmen, please note that there is a family of spiders (Pholcidae) that closely resemble harvestmen and are often mistaken for them. Although these spiders are not dangerous, like most spiders they can bite if mishandled.

Flies

Q *Help! Our home has been invaded with gnats. They are always flying around us, especially in the kitchen and bathrooms. They are very hard to whack because they are so fast and for that reason would be difficult to spray. How can we eliminate them from inside our home?*

From a reader in Stockton, CA

A The secret to getting rid of these small flies (gnats) is to determine which species you have. There are at least five common flies that could be the culprit and a positive identification is essential if they are to be eliminated.

Fruit flies are small, about $1/8''$ long, including wings. They are easily recognized by their red eyes. (You will need a magnifying glass to see the eyes of a gnat!) Fruit flies breed in ripened fruit and vegetables as well as moist, decaying organic materials. A piece of banana kicked behind an appliance can breed hundreds of fruit flies in a very short time.

Humpbacked flies, or coffin flies, are about the same size as fruit flies but have a distinctive humpbacked appearance. They breed in moist, decaying organic matter and can become a serious pest if left unchecked. They have been known to infest open wounds of people in hospitals and they often feed on cadavers; hence their other name, coffin flies.

Moth flies are very hairy which makes them distinctive. They breed in the gunk in drains and overflow drains in sinks and tubs and are often fairly common if the household has a septic tank.

Dung flies are small, black flies. The first segment of the last leg is enlarged (again, you need a magnifying glass), which is a distinctive characteristic of these flies. They breed in any decaying organic material and are often found in "not-very-clean" kitchen appliances. They may be found behind baseboards if mopping forces organic material into this area.

Fungus gnats are generally the culprits when household plants are overwatered. Most species are only about $1/16$" long and have long, thin legs. The best way to control these gnats is to let the houseplants dry out almost to the point of wilting. The larvae in the soil will desiccate, ending the cycle.

As you can see, it is important to determine which fly is the problem.

Q *I have very small flies or gnats in my living room. What are they and how do I get rid of them?*

From a reader in Boston, MA

A You indicated on the phone that you had a lot of houseplants. I believe the insects are dark-winged fungus gnats. These little gnats breed in damp soil. The best solution is to let the plants dry out almost to the point of wilting and then re-water. By this time the fly larvae will be dead. The adults only live a short time and cannot breed in dry soil. Try not to let the soil remain damp or the fungus gnats will return.

No pesticides are necessary for these little flies. You can also put a layer of sand on the soil which will prevent the flies from laying their eggs in the soil.

Q *I am finding little worm-like things in my kitchen. I can't find the source and my exterminator has no idea what they are. Can you help?*

From a reader in Albuquerque, NM

A When I talked to you, you indicated that the "worms" didn't have any legs and they were narrower at one end. These are undoubtedly fly larvae or maggots. Occasionally a mouse or bird or some other little animal gets stuck in a wall, false ceiling, or other inaccessible place; it dies and subsequently attracts blow flies. What you are seeing are probably blow fly larvae. They leave the area of the dead animal when the carcass is consumed and crawl around looking for other food sources. As the carcass is consumed, the reproductive process of the blow fly will stop and you will not see any more larvae.

Q *We have these small gnat-like flies all over the place and can't figure out where they are coming from. Can you identify them and give us a suggestion?*

From a reader in Cedar Crest, NM

A The flies you brought in are pomace flies, also known as fruit flies or vinegar flies. Usually they breed in decaying fruit or vegetables, but they can also breed in a refrigerator pan, a clogged drain, or even a soured mop. If you use a string mop you may force water with bits of food under a baseboard and that may be enough to provide harborage for these flies. Check all of the areas mentioned and I am sure you will find the source, which can then be eliminated. The use of pesticides is not necessary for the control of pomace flies. You can catch the adult flies by trapping them. Use a quart jar provided with a funnel to allow the flies entry and bait the jar with a piece of banana sprinkled with yeast. This will collect the flies for about two weeks, at which time it should be replaced if the flies are still present.

Q *We have a cabin north of Taos that gets infested with flies every fall and spring. What are they and what can we do to control them?*

From a reader in Albuquerque, NM

A You have cluster flies. The adult flies can be a serious problem in office buildings when the flies migrate into the buildings during the fall and they often concentrate in the upper stories of the building. Frequently, people find large piles of dead cluster flies in mountain vacation homes that are unoccupied when the flies emerge in the spring.

Cluster flies do not feed on garbage or dead animals and do not breed in buildings. They are parasites of earthworms. When they migrate into buildings in the winter they seek out areas to spend the winter, usually wall voids or attics. They emerge from their hiding places in the spring and migrate toward windows in large numbers.

Once inside it is virtually impossible to control cluster flies. The best you can do is vacuum up as many as possible. The best control is to prevent them from entering the building by sealing all areas of the buildings, particularly on the south and west sides. Caulking, screening, and any similar efforts will help. Pesticides are not necessary to control cluster flies.

Q *I have horses and have not found a way to control black flies around the yard. Do you have any suggestions?*

I use fly traps for the house flies, but it still doesn't seem to make much of a dent. Any other suggestions? Any info you have will be helpful.

From a reader in Albuquerque, NM

A Black flies are day-feeding, blood-sucking flies that cause extreme discomfit in horses and other animals. The pain and itching following the bite suggests the presence of an allergen, which is injected while the fly is feeding. Deaths due to toxemia or anaphylactic shock along with blood loss and suffocation by inhalation of flies are all on record.

The location of feeding on the animal depends on the species of black fly involved; some feed on body areas devoid of hair, some by crawling down the mantle, and others by feeding inside the ears. The bites can cause lesions and irritation that can last for months.

Individual animal treatment with available insecticides is effective against the ear-feeding black flies but is not effective against the others. Noninsecticide treatment consists of an application of a petroleum jelly to the ears of horses, which protects them for about 3 days. One method that has proven effective in reducing black-fly attack on horses is the larviciding of streams where they breed.

Q *I just returned from a plant collection trip in the northern part of the New Mexico where I was mercilessly attacked by what I was told are "no-see-ums." What are these micro monsters? To what family do they belong? What is their life history? Do females require a blood meal like mosquitoes? How long do they live and how long are they active? Is it true that no insect repellent known to man will deter these creatures? Or does Avon Skin-So-Soft really work, and if so, why?*

From a reader in Albuquerque, NM

A No-see-ums are also referred to as biting midges, punkies, gnats, and moose flies, among other things. They belong to the fly family Ceratopogonidae and are among the smallest flies known, reaching only about a half a millimeter in length, which enables them to pass right through screen doors.

Punkies feed on all sorts of animals besides humans, including horses, cattle, sheep, poultry, reptiles, and many others and can transmit some serious pathogenic nematodes, viruses, and protozoans.

Only the female bites and her scissor-like mandibles make the bite a painful experience. She requires a blood meal to reproduce. The eggs and larvae of punkies are extremely prone to desiccation so the female lays her eggs in an almost aquatic environment, such as along the shores of streams, creeks, or rivers; around stock tanks; holes in trees; and very wet soil. Males live only to mate and become sexually fertile when they are only 8 hours old and start to lose their virility by the time they reach the advanced age of 24 to 36 hours. Female no-see-ums have been observed feeding on their mates while mating.

I am not aware of any good repellent for these flies except Avon Skin-So-Soft, which apparently works for a short while. I have heard that in some parts of the world, people rub cow dung on themselves to ward off these flies, but that may be a little unpleasant, especially to anyone standing nearby.

Some recent tests of mosquito repellents demonstrated that Avon Skin-So-Soft does work marginally as a mosquito repellent. Unfortunately, it also acts as an attractant as it brings the mosquitoes in before they are repelled. Also, it doesn't last very long, which leaves us with two conclusions: Don't walk around with someone who is using Avon SSS if you are not using it, and be prepared to reapply it about every half hour or so.

Q *We live near a dairy and generally get a lot of flies at different times of the year. Is there anything we can do to keep them under control besides chasing them around with a can of bug spray?*
From a reader in Belen, NM

A Flies, along with their relatives the mosquitoes, have caused more human and animal deaths than any other insects. The common housefly itself is suspected of carrying sixty-five human and animal diseases. It has been linked to outbreaks of cholera, anthrax, dysentery, tuberculosis, typhoid fever, plague, yaws, leprosy, and tapeworm. The Centers for Disease Control and Prevention consider the common housefly a greater danger to humans than any other species because of its close association to us and its filthy habits.

The main way to control flies is through sanitation. However, when you live near a dairy as you do, you will get flies no matter what you do. Here are a couple of hints. You can use baited jars outside to collect and dispose of some of them before they get in. Commercial flytraps are available but you can make some traps by simply folding a piece of stiff paper into a cone and inserting it in a jar. Bait the jar with raw hamburger, fish, or almost anything that is decaying or disgusting and you will catch flies. There are electric flytraps available that will also kill a large number of flies.

Flypaper is still available but is limited in its effectiveness. Do not use pest strips indoors as they constantly release toxic vapors in the air. Many contain chlorpyrifos, a suspected carcinogen that the Environmental Protection Agency is considering banning (none too soon in my opinion).

Flies are drawn to light. You can darken a room they are in and then open a door. As they gather on the screen they will be easy to kill, or open the screen and they will fly out. At night before you go to bed, close all the drapes and blinds, leaving a narrow slit in one of them. In the morning the flies will be torpid on the bare strip of glass and will be easy to dispatch. Do not use insecticides on flies as many of them are becoming resistant to the chemicals (and you are not). You can easily kill them by spraying them with rubbing alcohol. If course, nothing beats a fly swatter. Wash the fly swatter with hot, soapy water and allow it to air-dry to prevent contamination.

Q *I have these little gnats flying all around my bar. I can't seem to get rid of them and I set off foggers once a week. Any suggestions?*
From a reader in Ft. Wayne, IN

A Yes, forget the foggers. These little insects are fruit flies and they are living on fermenting fruit and liquor that has spilled. It is very important to do a thorough cleaning after closing each night. If you have wooden slats for the bartenders to stand on they should be picked up and the floor cleaned under them. Fruit should be put away every night and the bar should be cleaned with soap and water nightly. You can trap the flies after you have removed their food source by placing a couple of bottles that are half filled with vinegar and half with water with a dash of dish soap in several areas around the bar. The fruit flies will be attracted to this mixture and drown in the bottles. Pesticides are never necessary for fruit flies.

Q *I service one of the school districts in New Mexico and they have found a number of little "worms" swimming around in several of the commodes. What are they and what can we do about them?*
From a pest control operator in Albuquerque, NM

A The "worms" you brought in are the larval (maggot) stage of the black scavenger fly (family Sepsidae). The larvae live in excrement and various types of decaying organic materials. The adults are common flies that are often found near materials where the larvae breed. Since it is not likely that the adult flies would have access to the contents of the commode or sewer line, I suspect that there may be a plumbing problem at the school. Possibly there is a break in the line somewhere giving the adult flies access to the excrement. The larvae will easily breed in the sewer sludge and will work their way back into the commode. As a pest control operator there is nothing you can do about this problem except to advise the school officials. You certainly can't spray any pesticides into the commodes to kill the maggots. Once it is determined where the adult flies have access to the sewer sludge, then they can be stopped at that point by repairing any leaks in the pipes.

Q *I have these little bugs in my bathroom and I can't figure out where they are coming from. Can you help?*

From a reader in Raleigh, NC

A The insect you brought in is a moth fly. It is a very small, hairy fly that breeds in the gunk buildup in drainpipes and overflow drains. While they are harmless, there is some evidence that they can spread diseases because of the decaying material they breed in. The best method of control is to keep your drains as clean as possible by using a drain cleaner periodically. You can also fill up your sink with hot soapy water to get to the moths that might be breeding in the overflow drains.

The notorious sand flies that plagued our troops during the Gulf War are relatives of the common moth fly. While sand flies are capable of biting, moth flies are not. No pesticides are necessary to control moth flies.

Q *This may sound like a silly question, but what purpose do flies have besides to just aggravate us?*

From a reader in St. Louis, MO

A Flies are one of the most important groups of insects on the planet. They are found almost everywhere. There are flies that breed in water, in brine, and even in oil. They bore into the stems, leaves, and fruits of various plants and some species construct galls on plants. You can find flies living in or flying around flowers, sap, dead animals, rotting plant material, feces, garbage, the sap of trees, and many other places. No animal, with the exception of humans, is responsible for a greater loss of human life than flies. More than 50 percent of the world's population becomes infected with disease via fly-borne pathogens or parasites.

The good news is that the larvae of many species of flies are either predaceous or parasitic on many pest insects. Many other species break down decomposing organic material and, in fact, are exceeded only by bacteria and fungi in the role of processing dead plant and animal material. Some flies aid law enforcement officers in determining the time of death in homicides through the science of forensic entomology.

There are approximately 100,000 species of flies worldwide and about 17,000 live in the United States.

Jerusalem Crickets
(a.k.a. Child-of-the-Earth)

Q *Is the child-of-the-earth dangerous and what is it exactly?*
From a reader in Tucson, AZ

A The child-of-the-earth is more correctly called a Jerusalem cricket. Although quite common, they are shy and nocturnal in their habits and they are rarely seen. Its striking appearance is due to its round, "bald" head with markings that form, with a little imagination, a smiling face. The Navajo Indians call it *who-she-tsinni,* meaning "old man bald head."

While many people are afraid of Jerusalem crickets and even believe them to be venomous, they are actually very harmless, although a large one can give you a painful nip if you pick it up.

They should be left alone, as they do no harm.

Q *Regarding Jerusalem crickets, I agree with your answer how we misjudge people by their appearance. I have used these misjudged crickets for fishing bass and they work great.*

Since I moved to central California I can't seem to locate them anywhere, above or under ground. Is there somewhere I can buy them? Or are they illegal to sell? The best live bait I've ever used. Thanks,

From a reader in Santa Maria, CA

A I have never heard of using Jerusalem crickets for bass bait but I can see where they would work. Unfortunately, they are difficult to breed and there really isn't a market for them so I have no idea where you can buy them. It wouldn't be illegal to sell them, just not practical.

Maybe you can start a new industry!

Millipedes

Q *They are throughout the house but firmly entrenched in the bathroom, kitchen, and bedroom. They are small, black, and crawl from the baseboards toward the ceilings. There are hundreds of them on the shelf above the fireplace. We have tried a couple of sprays and are currently working with Raid for house and garden.*

From a reader in Los Alamos, NM

A You sent me some specimens as I requested and they are harmless little duff millipedes. I assume you have pines or pinyons in your yard or a lot of bark mulch. Outside they live under the bark of trees or in bark mulch. These little millipedes occasionally crawl into homes in large numbers, as you are aware. They will not be able to get the moisture they require in your home and will eventually just die out. There is no good chemical control for them. I would suggest just wiping them up with a sponge and soapy water. Between the two pest control companies and what you have sprayed, I don't think you need any more chemicals in your house.

Q *I read your column in the* Vero Beach Press Journal *every week and have found it most informative. I have a problem. I have been invaded by a small worm, about ¹/₂" in length. They are brown/black in color with no distinctive markings. They have many legs and have made my life miserable. They have been*

*found on my patio, in the swimming pool, in the bathroom, and
in the kitchen. I have asked the exterminator if there was something he could do to eradicate them. He gave me the name of the
bug but I cannot remember what it was; he said he had nothing
that would keep these pesky little "worms" under control. They
seem to be heading for water. We have had a very dry spell in this
area of Florida recently, and I think that is why they are invading
my home at this point. Interestingly enough, my neighbor across
the street is not bothered with them at all. Why do I have them
and what can I do to get rid of them?*

From a reader in Vero Beach, FL

A The pests that you described are very common millipedes.
Most millipedes feed on decaying plant material, but they
may eat plant roots or enter fruits and tubers in and on damp
soil. To control the millipedes outside, you can remove their
hiding places such as rocks, heavy mulch, boards, or anything else they can hide under. You should also water early
in the morning, which allows the ground to dry out, instead
of watering at night, which causes the soil to remain wet all
night. Wet soil is conducive to millipede activity. You can
also drench the soil with tobacco tea, which is nothing more
than boiling tobacco in water. Nicotine is an effective pesticide and will kill the millipedes. Millipedes that enter the
home should be vacuumed up, as they will die quickly. Door
sweeps should probably be installed on the doors to prevent
them from entering the home.

Mites/Chiggers

Q *I am from the Midwest and have heard about chiggers. I want to
know something about them and if fingernail polish works to
remove them.*

From a reader in Indiana

Q *My yard is giving us all a chigger problem. What can be done so
that we can walk in our yard or be in the yard, and not be "eaten
up" with chigger bites? We are desperate for help.*

From a reader in Iowa

A Chiggers are the immature stage of a mite that feeds on insects in the adult stage. They are a common nuisance over much of the United States. Chiggers crawl up the pant legs of unsuspecting people and work their way down into hair follicles where they feed for awhile. They inject a substance that dissolves tissue causing the itch they are famous for and which may persist for weeks.

Fingernail polish is of no use in suffocating the chiggers because they are probably gone by the time you notice the itch. A good remedy for stopping the itch is to apply vinegar to the area of the bite.

The only solution that I am aware of that will kill chiggers besides pesticides is insecticidal soap. This product is labeled for a wide variety of insects and other arthropods and chiggers are among the critters it is labeled to control. Read the label before using insecticidal soap or any pesticide for that matter.

When in chigger territory you should wear high shoes or boots and be cautious about sitting on the ground. Mosquito repellent can be helpful.

Q *Will cleaning my heating ducts eliminate dust mites from my house?*

From a reader in Albuquerque, NM

A I doubt if you have dust mites. They have received a lot of attention in the last twenty years or so because their feces and associated debris can be allergenic. Dust mites, however, are not a problem in parts of the country with little humidity.

Dust mites develop on bacteria associated with skin flakes, hair, and other human debris that makes up about 80 percent of household lint. These bacteria require a minimum of 60-percent humidity to survive. Needless to say these conditions are rarely met and never sustained in the Southwest. The bacteria can't survive here and neither can the mites.

The fact that dust mites do not occur in the Southwest has not stopped several companies from trying to instill panic about them. Most common are certain businesses involved in steam cleaning and vacuuming ductwork. It is ludicrous that these companies claim dust mites live in something as dry as a heating duct. They may be able to remove the dust bunnies, but there are no dust mites.

Q *I read your column in the* Detroit News, *and hope you can help me. I have clover mites in my kitchen and have tried two bombs and different sprays but have had no luck. I called the extension service in Mt. Clemens; I was told to forget about them, that they will go away by themselves. After three months their numbers seem to be unchanged, and I want to get rid of them. Hope you can help me?*

From a reader in Detroit, MI

A Clover mites are resistant to most pesticides so you won't have much luck spraying and bombing the house. These mites originate in the grass or vegetation outside and generally enter the home by crawling under a door or window. The best way to prevent them in the future would be to cut the grass and shrubbery back from the foundation at least 3 feet and fill the area with loose, fine sand. Clover mites won't cross this kind of barrier.

The mites that are already in the house can be wiped up with a sponge and hot, soapy water. You can also place tape on the windows in the rooms where the mites are entering, which will entrap the ones crawling under the windows.

Q *My dog has demodectic mange. My vet says there isn't any cure. What do you know about mange?*

A Your veterinarian is correct. Demodectic mange generally affects dogs with a weakened immune system. Young puppies or older dogs suffering from malnutrition, parasitic infections, or other types of debilitating diseases are particularly susceptible.

Mange is caused by the presence of very small, elongated follicle mites belonging to the family Demodicidae and the genus *Demodex*. They are about $1/250$th of an inch in length. The shape of these mites allows them to live in hair follicles, and often several mites in all stages can be found in a single hair follicle. They reproduce fast as the entire development period from egg to adult may take less than a month.

Bats, rodents, carnivores, horses, cattle, rabbits, monkeys, and kangaroos all have their own species of follicle mites.

Humans can have two species of these mites. One infests the hair follicles and the other can be found in the sebaceous glands around the eyes, nose, and mouth. Most people have these mites, albeit they don't realize it as the mites cause no harm or discomfort.

Q *Last year some of my fruit trees were diagnosed with eriophyid mites. What are they and how do I control them?*

From a reader in Sonoma, CA

A Eriophyid mites, which are found on a wide variety of trees and shrubs, rarely cause any significant damage.

Because of their small size, they are difficult to see. On some plants, large populations develop, causing the leaves to turn a rusty color. Most eriophyid mites spend the winter as adults under the scales of buds or within galls. They become active early in the spring and are usually present in high numbers by early summer. There are multiple generations over the course of a year.

Eriophyid mites are eaten by a number of arthropods, including predatory mites, predatory thrips, minute pirate bugs, and many other small predators associated with vegetation.

🐛 **The following exchange concerned grain mites and a poorly trained exterminator's attempt to control them.**

Q *Several days ago my housemate discovered that the microwave was covered with what he thought was white flour. He thought I was making bread . . . carelessly. Then, on closer inspection, he noticed that they were moving. With a magnifying glass and a flashlight we found them everywhere in the kitchen, in some areas concentrated to a dozen per square inch. It has been damp and there was a recent break in a kitchen pipe, leaving the area under the house very damp. These insects are white, probably about $1/32$ of an inch or smaller. We have found them also in the adjoining room, all over the TV. We cleaned with a bleach* *solution but they kept coming. What are they and what should we do?*

P.S.: I do not like to use insecticides.

From a reader in Richmond, VA

A They sound like springtails but I can't be sure without seeing them. If they are springtails you should be able to kill them by wiping them up with soap and water. If you would like to send some to me to positively identify, I may be able to help.

Reader's response

Thank you so much for replying to my e-letter. This is what has happened since then. A neighbor who has some college-level education about bugs came over.

She had a good microscope and we identified them as mites and then by searching on the Internet, we narrowed the possibilities to grain mites. We then wiped them up with hot soapy water as recommended by our source and confirmed now by you as a good tactic. Alas, they were undaunted, and returned within minutes. We went at it for several days, even using a shop vac, when my housemate lost patience and we agreed to talk and listen to an organic exterminator.

My housemate told her to go ahead and she used tree oils and pyrethrins. We have left the counters and cabinets alone for today figuring that the residual of the chemical would continue to work.

My Response

A dust called Drione, which is made from silica gel, is good for grain mites, as I am sure the pest control person mentioned (or should have). You have to get it in cracks and crevices where the mites can hide. If the exterminator comes back, mention Drione and ask him or her to use it.

Reader's response

Once again, thank you for your quick response to my emails. If I fail to reciprocate, it is because I am compelled to use the terminal at my local library. . . . My housemate tells me that the exterminator suggested a chemical fog and remembered it phonetically as "resmethrin." I am very suspicious of these chemicals and do not use them myself even as a carpenter. . . . I work around wasps and bees; they have never (knock on wood) stung me and I just stay calm around them.

Will the dust you mentioned, Drione, get rid of these tiny insects quickly? Is this product "resmethrin" questionable for use around humans (and dogs)? Again, thanks so much for your help in all of this.

My response

I have no use for resmethrin and I can't believe an exterminator would suggest fogging for mite control. The Drione will work fine. Forget the fogging and hire a new exterminator.

Pantry Pests

Q *I finally arrived in Boston after a long and arduous trip. I never thought I'd have another bug question for you so soon. . . . My dad and sister and uncle have these small moths, which I think are called "spaghetti moths." They are all over the place, probably in the hundreds, and seem to eat cereal, etc. How on earth do we get rid of them? I told my family about you, and said you're the bug expert, and you'd certainly know what to do—if anyone does. Any suggestions?*

From a reader in Boston, MA

A I am not sure what a "spaghetti moth" is specifically, but I assume it is one of the moths collectively known as "stored-product pests." There are a number of species but the Indian meal moth, *Plodia interpunctella,* is the most common. In addition to cereals, it will feed on nuts, seeds, candy, dried pet foods, spices, dried fruits and vegetables, and many other foodstuffs.

The adult moth is about $1/2$" long, and generally gray in color with bronze-colored wing tips. Feeding damage is done by larvae, which are usually light colored with a dark head.

Eggs are laid by the adult moths near suitable food, such as in cracks or folds in packaging, behind shelves, and under baseboards of pantries. The newly hatched larvae are capable of penetrating into loosely closed packages where they begin feeding. Development from egg to adult is fairly rapid under ideal conditions and the adult moth can lay between 200 and 400 eggs in her lifetime of several weeks.

Carefully inspect all food items and throw away anything that you suspect is contaminated. Pay particular attention to items that have not been used in a long time. Also check areas of spilled foods, including sites that may not be obvious, such as under refrigerators and stoves.

Thoroughly clean all of these areas with hot water and a strong detergent. Pay attention to the back of the shelves in the pantry and the baseboards on the floor as the larvae may be hiding in these areas. Never use pesticides as they will only provide limited control and may be more hazardous than a few bugs in the cereal.

Finally, contact the manager of the store where you shop and let him/her know of your problem. Chances are that you brought these moths in with some food you bought and the store or its supplier is probably the origin of the problem.

Q *We have little beetles in our pantry and my exterminator wants to spray the shelves. Is there another way?*
From a reader in Raleigh, NC

Q *The dog food in my garage is covered with little black bugs. Where did they come from and how do I get rid of them?*
From a reader in Vero Beach, FL

Q *In our kitchen and pantry we have little black bugs about $1/4$" long and very skinny. I think they are weevils. They get into even unopened packages.*
What does it take to get rid of the little bugs?
From a reader in Albuquerque, NM

A You have what are collectively known as stored-product pests (SPPs). There are a number of different insects that infest grains, breads, cereals, and other foods. Most are beetles or moths. You have to inspect all of the food in the pantry and throw away everything that is infested.

The pantry needs to be completely cleaned with special attention given to the area where the shelf joins the wall as food particles can collect there. Also concentrate on the floor along the wall. After you have discarded the infested food and thoroughly cleaned the pantry, there are a few other guidelines you should follow to prevent a reinfestation.

- Do not put exposed food on the shelves. Place in containers with tight-fitting lids (plastic bags are not adequate).
- Regularly clean shelves, bins, and all other locations where there is any possibility of food particles accumulating.
- Do not mix old and new foodstuffs. If the old material is infested, the insects will quickly infest the new.
- Clean old containers before filling them with fresh food. They may be contaminated and can cause a new infestation.
- Do not purchase broken or damaged packages of food products even if they are cheaper. They are more likely to be infested.
- Store bulk foods in containers with tight-fitting lids.
- Keep storage areas dry as moisture is conducive to the development of SPPs and dryness discourages them.
- SPPs can breed in rodent bait. Another good reason not to use rodenticides in the home.

Q *We occasionally have insects in our bulk grain at our place of business. Is there any way to solve this problem with pesticides?*
From a reader in Oklahoma

A Most insects won't infest grain when the humidity is less than 6 percent. One exception is the Mediterranean meal moth, which can survive in as little as 1-percent humidity. A dehumidifier in your storage area may be helpful. You can also dry the grain by pouring it slowly through the air past a fan or past an electric heater with a strong blower. The blowing has the added benefit of removing broken kernels, chaff, and fungal spores.

You can also add diatomaceous earth to the storage bin.

This powder will kill any insects by disrupting their skins, causing dehydration. The grains should be thoroughly rinsed before using. Be sure to use the grade of diatomaceous earth specially made for treating grain and not the type used in swimming pool filters; the latter is not edible, because it has been heated to 2,000° F and has crystallized like glass.

Q *Help! These bugs are all over my kitchen and bathrooms (a new home). There is a farmer's field (beans, corn) beyond my property line and my neighbor just had his quackgrass torn up and yard reseeded. I believe I noticed these bugs before he tore his grass up. What are they? Why are they in my house? And, how can I get rid of them?*

From a reader in Cedar Lake, IN

A The bugs you included with your letter are silken fungus beetles (Cryptophagidae). The adults and larvae of fungus beetles are found in moldy plant and animal material, in flowers, in fungi, and in moldy grains. They are frequently found in houses, cellars, warehouses, and other indoor environments where conditions are conducive to them. Many of the fungus beetles are found in association with stored foods where they live on the spores of molds.

Control of these beetles requires finding where they are breeding and eliminating the source. Check your pantry for spillage or for stored food items that you may not have used for awhile and that may have become moldy.

Q *I live just outside Edmonton, Alberta, Canada. Our house is made of wood, the insulation is blown in the walls, and the interior walls are cedar planks. I do see these beetles outside occasionally (in the garage).*

They are approximately 1/8" to 1/4" long. Let me know if this is enough information. If not, I will pop a few in the mail to you.

From a reader in Edmonton, Alberta, Canada

A I received the beetles in the mail today and they are larder beetles *(Dermestes lardarius).* Larder beetles feed on stored ham, bacon, meats, cheese, dried museum specimens, trophies, stored tobacco, dried fish, dog biscuits, and other organic material. They can tunnel slightly in wood and can even penetrate lead and tin in search of food. They have been known to attack newly hatched chickens and ducklings.

You obviously have something that they are eating in your house or garage. It is important that you find the source of food and dispose of it. Once you do that the beetles will be gone.

Silverfish

Q Hi Richard, After purchasing my new home and working around in the attic I was surprised to see the vermiculite ceiling insulation was infested with silverfish. I know you often find this insect near moist, dark areas, but the attic is dry. My only thought was they are feeding on the vermiculite, so it is my plan to have all the insulation replaced with fiberglass. My question is: After removing the insulation should I have the area treated? And what should I look for in terms of exterminators and what safe pesticides they use for this insect? Thanking you in advance!!

From a reader in Richmond, VA

A Silverfish can be controlled with a product called Niban Bait, which is made from boric acid. The bait can be placed in the attic under the insulation. You can also place the bait under sinks, behind and under furniture, and any other places where silverfish might forage. Make sure you place the bait out of reach of children and pets and also read the label very carefully.

Spiders

Q My boyfriend brought home a tarantula he found on the road. Is it dangerous? Can we keep it? If so, how do we take care of it?

From a reader in Edgewood, NM

A The tarantula is probably a male of the common species known as the "Mexican blond tarantula." It is not dangerous and you can probably keep it for a short while. Males are frequently seen on roads as they are wandering around looking for females, which live in burrows. While females may live many years, males do not. Your tarantula will probably die within a few months whether you let him go or keep him. If you keep him, feed him crickets and put a small jar lid in the terrarium with a piece of sponge soaked in water.

Q *There is a huge brown spider with horns in my backyard. It appears to be as big as my fist. It looks ferocious. What should I do?*
From a reader in Albuquerque, NM

A That is a female pumpkin spider, sometimes called the cat-faced spider. It is large, tan or brown, and has protuberances on the abdomen that could be called horns. She isn't quite as large as your fist but is a good-sized spider. They make large orb-shaped webs, usually in trees or bushes but occasionally under the eaves of a house. These spiders are quite harmless and in fact they should be considered beneficial as they eat a large number of insects, including several pest species. Pumpkin spiders should never be killed. If you have to move her, you can place her in a jar and relocate her to a tree or shrub where she will be out of the way.

Q *We thought you would enjoy these pictures of our pumpkin spider. We have had more fun watching her over the past two months. Just as you said, she disappeared the first of November. Now we are curious to learn more about pumpkin spiders. Do you suppose Pumpkin will come back? Has she had her babies? We never saw any evidence of them.*

We have certainly stirred up a lot of interest in pumpkin spiders! We have friends all over asking about our newest pet. Thanks for your interest and your help.
From a reader in Albuquerque, NM

A She won't return next year. If she successfully laid eggs, some of them may mature and you should see one or more of her progeny next fall.

Spiders are very interesting animals and should never

be killed. The pumpkin spider belongs to the spider family Araneidae and the order Arachnida. Greek mythology tells of Arachne, a girl so confident in her weaving ability that she challenged the goddess Athena to a contest. Arachne won and so angered Athena that she (Arachne) killed herself. Athena made amends by turning Arachne's body into a spider so that she may weave for eternity the most beautiful of webs of the finest silk. The spider order arachnida is named in honor of this girl.

It is also said that Robert the Bruce, an early king of Scotland, while hiding in a cave, observed the diligence, perseverance, and determination of an orb-weaving spider as it went about the process of spinning her web against seemingly insurmountable odds as she endured the onslaught of wind-blown rain to complete her task. Each time the web was damaged, it was rebuilt. It was this persistence in the face of defeat that inspired Robert the Bruce to continue his fight against the English, which eventually led to the independence of Scotland from England.

Q *My daughter was bitten (tonight) by a small spider. It caused a small reaction (red blotch) on her arm that quickly dissipated, but you can still see it. I have the spider in a glass. It is about the size of the head of a thumb tack, legs and all, the body smaller of course. The body has a brown-reddish head with a brown-gray abdomen. The legs are light rust-brown.*

We are not really worried about it, having read that your chances of dying from a poisonous spider bite are the same as getting killed by a flying champagne cork. But, if the description rings a bell, we would appreciate your feedback.

From a reader in Albuquerque, NM

A The spider you brought to my office is a small sac spider. Most species aren't seriously venomous but they will nip you if they are touched. The species you brought in is common in the area (I have found a number of them in my house and I have been bitten). I never recommend spraying pesticides for spiders. As sac spiders are hunters and spend a lot of time running around on the floor, it may be helpful to place some sticky traps (glueboards) along the wall to intercept them. Of course, you have to put these traps where kids and pets can't entangle themselves. As a side note, after opening the jar to look at your spider I neglected to put the lid back on. She is presently living somewhere in my office.

Q *I saw your column in the newspaper and hoped you could help me. I am wondering what kind of a spider it is that lives in my house. It is usually small—about ¹/₂" long, with a brown rear body and a reddish front body. It seems to have prominent fangs and long front legs, and usually runs for cover on the bathroom or kitchen floor, usually seen at night. My son found one on the outside wall of the house that was about twice as long, or 1".*

I was mostly wondering if it was a brown recluse, but if not, can you tell from my description what it is?

From a reader in Texas

A The spider you describe is quite common and quite harmless even if it is very intimidating looking. It doesn't have a common name, but its scientific name is *Dysdera crocota*. This interesting spider feeds almost exclusively on pillbugs (roly-polys). They normally live under stones or other objects on the ground where pillbugs live and their long "fangs" are an adaptation for feeding on the pillbugs. These little spiders should never be killed but unfortunately many are because of the indiscriminate use of pesticides, especially when people spray chemicals all around their foundation.

This method of "pest control," in which the outside foundation of a building is sprayed, is not environmentally sound and should be discouraged whenever possible. For every so-called "pest" the pest control industry claims they are controlling with this practice, I can name a dozen harmless and even beneficial organisms they are killing, such as the *Dysdera crocata* mentioned above. If you have a pest control service and they are spraying around your home, ask them to stop, as it is probably doing more harm than good.

Q *We found a large, black spider in our living room the other day and it doesn't appear to be a black widow. It isn't living in a web. Could you tell me what it is if I bring it to your office?*

From a reader in Corrales, NM

A The spider you brought in is a burrowing wolf spider. Wolf spiders are active this time of year now that the evenings are getting warmer. It entered your home inadvertently while looking for prey. It will be much happier outside (as I am sure you will be too) so the best way to solve this minor problem is to put a jar or glass over it, slide a stiff piece of paper under the glass entrapping the spider. Then invert the jar with the spider in it and put it outside. Wolf spiders are very beneficial and should never be killed.

Q *I have a four-story deck behind my building that is literally crawling with spiders—really, there must be hundreds. I'm constantly wiping off the webs, but they're usually back in the next day or two. I don't want to use a pesticide to remove them. Do you have any other recommendations? Is there anything I can spray them with that will drive them away?*

From a reader in San Francisco, CA

Q *Is there an easy way to get rid of cobwebs?*

From a reader in Napa Valley, CA

A Try spraying the webs with a mixture of meat tenderizer and water. Spider webs are made out of protein and will dissolve in meat tenderizer. Perhaps if you keep dissolving the webs, the spiders will feel unwelcome and move on. This will work on cobwebs also.

Q *Since the weather has started to warm up around here, we have been getting these black fuzzy spiders in our house. We have never seen any of these before so needless to say they've caught our eye and interest. They range from being about the size of your thumbnail to as large as a half dollar. Most of them are black with fuzzy legs, teal fangs, and an aggressive nature. When you go to look at them or accidentally stumble on one they turn and walk toward you. Some of them even will raise their front legs in a warning gesture. Others that seem to be from the same family have a small orange or red dot on the lower part of their back body. They do not have the teal fangs but they have the same body structure and characteristics of a hairy body and aggressive nature. Can you please write back and tell us if they are poisonous and what kind of spider they are?*

From a reader in Modesto, CA

A The spiders you describe are jumping spiders. Jumping spiders are active during the day and like sunshine. They walk with an irregular gait and can jump many times their own body length. Jumping spiders feed on flies and other insects and should be considered beneficial. One captive jumping spider fed on forty fruit flies in succession. These spiders have arguably the best eyesight among invertebrates as they can recognize prey or other spiders at a distance of 4" to 8".

As you mentioned they turn toward any movement trying to discern whether the movement is a source of food or a threat. Although they can bite like any other spider if handled, they should not be considered dangerous. If left alone, they will happily devour all of the flies they can find around your home.

Springtails

Q *I called in to your radio show last Friday, and you invited me to send you a bug sample to ID. I am desperate; my landlord has had an exterminator out three times, to no avail. They don't seem to respond to the spray at all!*

Here is the information I have: they are really minute (I hope you get something from these two samples). They have what looks like two thin antennae. They slither fairly fast; if I try to trap or kill one with a finger, they seem to be able to jump; not too high, but forward. They have been crawling on my bed, mostly; I see them when I am reading. They don't seem to be out much until evening. Can you tell me what these are, and how they need to be treated? Do I need to get rid of my bed, in case they're nesting in the mattress? What about nesting in my clothing, or in my cedar closet? My allergies have been much worse; do you think it is the spray, or could it be the critters?

I really, really appreciate any help you can give me. Please give me a call at your earliest convenience, and tell me what to do. I'm also enclosing a "trap" the exterminator gave me, but I don't think it's got any of these on it. I don't mind ants or flies as much, but these crawling things are terrible, and I can't sleep.

From a reader in Santa Fe, NM

A The insects you sent are springtails, one of the most numerous insects on the planet. They are also completely harmless. There are many species and they are often very common, sometimes numbering as many as 4,000 individuals per cubic foot. Springtails are capable of jumping because of a fork-like jumping organ, the furcula, which is folded forward on the underside of the abdomen, and the two prongs hook onto a clasp-like structure. When the furcula is tensed and suddenly released by the clasp, it strikes the ground with enough force to propel the springtails as much as 4" into the air.

They are most likely coming through a bedroom window or under a door. They usually live in moist soil but occasionally there are outbreaks of them and they move into homes. Check to see where they are coming in and spray all of the ones you see with soap and water. I would also suggest you wash your bedding to kill the few that may be on it. If your bed is near a window, you may want to move it until the outbreak subsides. It is absolutely amazing to me that there are still pest control companies that spray chemicals all over the place when they admittedly have no idea what they are spraying for. This lack of concern for the public is not only deplorable, it is borderline criminal. I suggest you have your landlord try to get his money back from the pest control company. Never, ever let exterminators spray pesticides if they are not absolutely sure what the target pest is. In this case, they had absolutely no idea. It is companies like this that give an honorable industry a bad name.

As for your allergies, I don't know what is causing them but I would guess one possibility is the pesticides that have needlessly been sprayed all over your home.

2

Destructive Bugs

Destructive bugs are insects that damage our possessions, including our homes. Some of them do superficial damage while others can have a major financial impact on people they affect. Most of the questions in this chapter are on termites, which is understandable as they can be very serious pests in homes.

Carpenter Bees

Q *I read with great interest your column regarding pesticides that work for carpenter ants, even though the reader had experienced lack of help from her exterminator. I am therefore writing to you in the hope that you have an answer regarding my problems with carpenter bees. We live in a house with cedar siding and a wooden storm door. It seems that the carpenter bees have decided that our home is their home. We have approached two exterminating companies who say they have no way to eliminate this problem. They did suggest that we spray the holes with canned air to "freeze" them. This did not work at all. Do you know of any pesticides that will work against carpenter bees? I have been considering trying to plug each hole with rat poisoning. We are getting desperate at this point.*

From a reader in Atlanta, GA

A As carpenter bees do not constitute a hazard through stinging and the fact that they are very valuable pollinators, they should not be killed if at all possible.

Where exposed wood is known to be a problem, keep it heavily coated with paints or varnish, if possible. Where damage is already underway, replace damaged wood or fill the holes with steel wool and staple on metal screening after the bees have emerged. If pesticides become necessary, consider using a pyrethrum-based material. Plug holes after treatment.

Carpenter bees have wood preferences such as southern yellow pine, white pine, California redwood, Douglas fir, and cypress. If there are any depressions in your siding, you should fill them as female carpenter bees are attracted to these areas. Holes should be plugged with steel wool and metal window screens. Many wood fillers are too soft to prevent carpenter bees from entering. Almond oil or essence has bee-repellent qualities, but you have to be careful as the ben-zeldehyde may contain certain other poisons that are toxic if swallowed or if the fumes are inhaled repeatedly. Almond oil or essence may be worth trying as a repellent during the active season until physical changes can be made.

Spraying the holes with canned air is the silliest suggestion I have heard. The lack of results is not surprising. Rat poison will not work either. Try the suggestions above that are relevant to your situation and you should be fine.

Carpet Beetles

Q *I have a recurring problem with carpet beetles. The exterminator comes out every five or six months to treat the same room. Does Albuquerque have a serious problem with these bugs?*
From a reader in Albuquerque, NM

A Albuquerque does not have any more carpet beetles than anywhere else in the area. The problem is that the larvae of carpet beetles are relatively resistant to pesticides. Another problem is that you may not be altering their living conditions so that they are not "disappearing" after the pesticide treatment but are living freely in other areas of the house. For instance, carpet beetles can live very well on the dust bunnies that gather under furniture. Only the larval stage of the beetle is destructive. The adults feed on the pollen of flowers, particularly white flowers. Here are some tips:

- Clean closets and dresser drawers regularly.

- Move heavy furniture at least once a month and thoroughly vacuum.
- Vacuum along baseboards and behind radiators. Vacuum draperies, valances, and upholstered furniture. Wrap the vacuum cleaner bag in a plastic bag and dispose of it.
- Vacuum and wash your pets' bedding as carpet beetles will thrive on a buildup of shed hairs.
- Avoid planting white flowers in your garden.
- Check any cut flowers for carpet beetles. The adults are small, round, and black or mottled in color.

You can trap carpet beetle larvae by putting a couple of slices of American cheese on a piece of soiled fabric in a corner of the room. The cheese will attract the larvae, which can then be disposed of by drowning.

These are all tips any competent pest management professional should have told you on his/her first visit to your home.

Clothes Moths

Q *We are having a problem with moths in one of our closets and our exterminator doesn't seem to be having any luck getting rid of them. He said they were codling moths. Can you help?*
From a reader in Rio Rancho, NM

A Unless you have an apple tree in your closet I would say his identification is wrong. You have clothes moths. Clothes moths are small, about a $1/2$" wingspan, buff-colored insects. The larvae feed on a variety of organic materials including wool, hair, feathers, furs, upholstered furniture, dead insects, dry dead animals, fish meals, and nearly all animal products. The adults do not feed. The adult female moth lays her eggs singly on the product the larvae will be feeding on, each female laying from 100 to 150 eggs. The eggs hatch in about five days into a larva. The larvae stage will last from six weeks up to four years depending on food and environmental factors. Development is influenced by humidity, the life cycle being the shortest in average room temperature, at about 75-percent humidity.

Cedar shavings probably will not work. The best method is to store the items in heat-sealed or otherwise completely sealed plastic bags when not in use. You should clean the material before storing it, or freeze it for a couple of days.

You need to treat the items known or suspected of being infested, and susceptible items should be stored in tight-fitting containers to prevent an infestation. Dry cleaning or storage with moth crystals will kill all stages of clothes moths. Pheromone traps are also helpful in collecting males and preventing them from breeding. You can make your own clothes-moth trap by dipping a couple of cotton balls in fish oil (tuna, sardines, etc.) and sticking them on a strip of fly paper and hanging them in a closet. Two strips per closet are sufficient and the fish oil will last about two weeks before it needs to be changed. The downside of this method is the fish oil odor.

Termites

Q *We live in the east mountains. Our house is 2.5 years old, single story, wood frame on heated slab, stucco; altitude 6,800 feet; setting, heavy clay-based, wooded meadow, junipers, pinyons. To the best of my knowledge, no termite treatment was done to the foundation, etc., during construction.*

People within about two miles were having some interior remodeling done on their house and the contractor uncovered "a severe bug problem." Exterminators were called in and the owners were told that the bugs were termites. A second opinion was sought and provided same guidance. Owners were told that many thousands of dollars will need to be spent to eliminate the problem.

What actions (if any) should I be taking to protect my investment? If you recommend inspections and/or treatment, how do I go about finding a reputable person and what should I expect to pay? Also, how frequently should I be doing what?

Thanks in advance.

From a reader in Tijeras, NM

A I would not be overly concerned about your neighbor's problem, but having said that, it wouldn't be a bad idea to have your house inspected every couple of years.

I am curious about your statement that the person with the termites is going to have to spend "many thousands of dollars" to eliminate the problem. I would hope that figure includes damage repair because the average termite job would be between one and two thousand dollars unless there are a lot of extenuating circumstances.

As for picking a termite company to do an inspection, just make sure the prospective inspector is properly licensed. If they find anything, don't sign a contract right away. Get several more opinions before you do anything. Determining a price for a termite treatment involves many factors so it is impossible to give a figure. The one-to-two-thousand-dollar figure I mentioned above should cover most homes unless they are unusually large or have other considerations that would make the treatment more difficult, and therefore more expensive.

Q *I just bought a home and the termite inspector found pieces of wood in the crawl space that had old termite damage. He recommended I have the house treated, but I am reluctant to have chemicals sprayed under the house. Is it necessary to treat the house under these circumstances?*

From a reader in Belen, NM

A If the termites are in or have been in loose wood debris and are not present in the structure itself, I don't recommend you have the house treated, especially if you have an aversion to pesticides. You may want to remove all of the loose wood and other material containing cellulose from the crawl space. Then you should have the crawl space inspected every year by a competent termite inspector to make sure the termites aren't entering the structure. If they do, then you can get it treated. Simply because there are termites or have been termites in the soil in the crawl space does not mean they will automatically enter the home. There are termites in yards all around homes and they do not necessarily enter the homes either.

The one valid reason there may be to treating the home

would be that the cost of a termite treatment goes up periodically and it may be less costly to do it now than in four or five years. Having said that, I would opt for waiting, as I do not like the use of pesticides as a "preventive" treatment. I would rather wait and use them only if and when they are absolutely necessary.

Q *We were going to bring some firewood in the house but it is covered with sawdust. Is this termites and will they get in the house?*
From a reader in Taos, NM

A No, the sawdust is not from termites. It is probably from one of several species of bark beetles or long-horned borers. Neither beetle will infest your house. The long-horned borer is generally a larger insect with exceptionally long antennae. Bark beetles are very small and will probably not even be noticed. The sawdust is caused by the larval stages of these insects. You can burn the firewood with the larvae in it. Do not spray firewood with pesticides as it will do little good and the residue may affect you when you burn the wood.

Q *I had several companies come out to my house and give me a bid for termite work. I was surprised at how far apart the bids were. How are these charges usually figured?*
From a reader in Santa Fe, NM

A Most companies charge by the linear foot of the house. The label rate for most termiticides is 4 gallons per 10 linear feet of foundation. Except in the case of a monolithic slab, both sides of the stem wall have to be treated. For instance, if your home measures 160 linear feet, you have to double that figure because you are treating the inside and the outside of the foundation. You now have 320 linear feet. Using the rate of 4 gallons per 10 linear feet, you can figure you will need at least 128 gallons of termiticide to treat your home. Most companies will use this figure to compute a price and then add additional work as necessary, such as drilling, patching, rodding, trenching, trap accession, etc. Make sure all of the bidders make a graph of your home and show you everything they are going to do in detail. Make sure you ask for references and check them. Guarantees are important, but it is also important to know that if the termite company isn't in business next year the guarantee will be worthless. It is also very important that they have a flow meter or some other way to measure the output of chemical so you know you are getting exactly the amount you need, no more and no less. If they don't have a method of measuring the chemical output, you may want to take that into consideration when making your decision. The substance of the proposal is far more important than the price.

Q *We have termites and one company suggested using bait stations while another said they didn't work and recommended pesticides. What do you think?*

From a reader in Albuquerque, NM

A I have been asked this question a number of times in the last couple of years and my opinion has not changed. However, because I do know many of the people in the pest control industry in New Mexico and because I don't want to appear prejudicial, I have contacted Cam Lay, a leading researcher in termite control from Clemson University in South Carolina and asked his opinion. He says:

> I think the bait systems are valuable tools but I don't think that they are the cure-all that they were initially marketed as. I initially said that when 5 or 6 years of successful field experience with them had accumulated that I would have more confidence. That's pest control operative experience, not experience with systems installed by Dow tech reps, University cooperators, graduate students, etc. We're now approaching that level of field experience in South Carolina, and I think I'm going to stick with my original opinion—valuable tools in some situations, not a cure-all, and probably not the best option in most situations. I'm a lot more comfortable with baits as an adjunct or supplemental technique than as a stand-alone. Even Nan-Yao Su, the guy that

developed Sentricon, will admit if you press him, that most of the baits are more effective if they're combined with a barrier treatment because the disruption of the established foraging pathways causes increased foraging and increases the likelihood that the stations will be detected.

The problems we're seeing fall into the usual two categories: human error and problems inherent to the systems themselves. A lot of the technological problems are essentially summarized on our bait-use disclosure form. I've listed some of the other concerns below.

The technician doesn't inspect the stations. Even if they're bar coded, some techs get behind and just swipe the bar code off the top of the station without actually inspecting. Some technicians fake the inspection reports. We've seen some discrepancies between the inspection data we get from Dow and the data we get from the applicator and the information provided by the homeowner. An egregious example is the guy with the two rottweilers in the backyard who says the tech has never been back (I believe him), even though the company's records indicate that every station has been inspected every 30 days. Bait systems are more effective if they are combined with a barrier treatment because the disruption of the established foraging pathway causes increased foraging and increases the likelihood that the stations will be detected.

The stations are put in the wrong places, laid out every 10' around the perimeter like a barrier, instead of placed in the areas the termites are likely to be.

The stations never get hit but the damage continues. I suspect that once termites establish a foraging pathway they don't deviate from it much. (It must be terribly expensive to build a tunnel everywhere you go, which leads quickly to the idea that once you have a tunnel built to a food source there's very little reason to expend calories doing a lot of extra looking around.) I've also seen situations where the infestation continues in the house despite "elimination" of the termites on the property. That's consistent with the idea of multiple colonies with interlocking but separate foraging pathways in an area. You kill five, but three more eat the house . . .

All of that said, I have seen some spectacular successes with the bait systems. I've also seen some spectacular failures. Like most everything, they depend heavily on the skill and thoroughness of the applicator. I'm not real happy that some companies have gone exclusively to the bait systems.

I concur with Cam Lay's assessment of the baits.

Q *Hi and thank you for your common sense and for your responsible attitudes toward the environment and toward human health. My husband and I live in the central valley of California and we have had or still have dry-wood termites in a limited portion of our house. The first termite inspector recommended that we use the tent and methyl bromide treatment very soon because they are going to outlaw that chemical very shortly. I have great reservations about fumigating my house with something like methyl bromide, and I hope I can find someone who recommends something else. Since the dry-wood termites may be in the wall studs and are difficult to detect, are there other methods that can work in these sites?*
From a reader in Stockton, CA

A He is right about outlawing methyl bromide and I won't miss it. I would never use MB in a house fumigation because it has a negative effect on too many household items. The fumigant I would recommend is sulfuryl fluoride (Vikane), which is normally the fumigant of choice for controlling dry-wood termites. I have used sulfuryl fluoride many times and it has no bad side effects and it is very effective.

There are firms in California that use heat to control dry-wood termites but I don't know if that method is perfected. If it was my house I would go with Vikane. Call some of the bigger companies and get three or four estimates. Forget the methyl bromide and forget the character that recommended it.

Q *I recently had my house inspected for termites. The inspector found termites in an expansion joint near my garage and said the house required treatment. I called another company for another opinion and they said the house did not require treatment. Who do I believe?*

From a reader in Los Lunas, NM

A The second guy is correct. Some companies try to sell termite jobs based on termites being found on the property and near the house but not in it. Termites found in areas outside of the structure that is being inspected should not be considered as infesting the structure. It is okay for the inspector to point out any termites on the property but it is wrong to suggest the home needs to be treated. There is no set distance (how far the termites are from the home) that is an industry standard to dictate treatment. Termites found even 6" from the foundation will not result in a treatment being "required." Similarly, termites found in fences and outbuildings should be reported but do not constitute a required treatment of the home.

Termites are common throughout the Southwest and are probably present in everyone's yard. I have termites in a dozen different locations around my home yet the house is not infested. One suggestion would be for the homeowner who is ordering an inspection to remove any wood-to-earth contact before the termite inspection is performed. Pull up any stakes in the yard near the home and even remove the wood from expansion joints in the sidewalk. Pick up and remove any boards or firewood near the foundation. If you have a crawl space, remove all wood, paper, and other debris before the inspection. If the termite inspector doesn't find any wood in contact with the soil, he won't find any termites in the yard and will limit his inspection to the structure of the house, as he should do anyway. If termites are found, always get several proposals before hiring someone to eradicate them.

Q *What other kinds of insects may be feeding on the wood in my house besides termites? My exterminator said "wood borers," but didn't seem to have any additional information. What is a wood borer?*

From a reader in Santa Fe, NM

A Wood borers are generally the larval stage of certain beetles. There are seven families of beetles in New Mexico that can be considered wood borers and some of them can be economically important. If you are buying a house it is a good idea to get it inspected for wood-destroying organisms before the purchase and it is very important that you hire an inspector who is intimately familiar with all the wood-destroying insects that may be encountered. Test your prospective inspector. If he/she isn't familiar with all of the families of wood-boring beetles than they aren't qualified to inspect your home. The seven beetle families are:

Powder-post beetles (Lyctidae)
These beetles predominantly attack hardwoods with high starch content and they can reinfest milled lumber. They are frequently found in imported wooden furniture, in artifacts, and in oak flooring.

Deathwatch beetles (Anobiidae)
Some species of anobiids attack both hardwoods and softwoods while other species attack only one or the other. A common place to find these beetles is in the joists and subflooring under homes. Thorough inspection of crawl spaces is necessary to locate these insects. They will reinfest milled lumber.

False powder-post beetles (Bostrichidae)
Bostrichids primarily attack softwood and rarely reinfest, although if there is enough moisture content in the wood, they may. They are occasionally found in the latillas in homes and have also been found to thoroughly infest log cabins.

Metallic wood Borers (Buprestidae)
Metallic wood borers, also known as flat-headed borers occasionally are found in vigas in new

homes. These beetles never reinfest and need no treatment.

Long-horned beetles (Cerambycidae)

Long-horned beetles, also known as round-headed borers, rarely reinfest but it is important to determine which species is present, because the black-horned pine borer can reinfest on occasion. These beetles are usually found in vigas in new homes.

Bark beetles (Scolytidae)

These are pests of minor significance in seasoned wood but very damaging in a forest. Bark-beetle damage is commonly found in houses built with infested wood. They do not reinfest.

Wood-boring weevils (Curculionidae)

These weevils attack sap and heartwood of hardwoods, softwoods and plywood. The amount of damage they do depends on the moisture content of the wood. They can reinfest.

Q *I built a house some years ago on my land in West Virginia, and used air-dried lumber from local saw mills. The lumber was sawn from a variety of native trees: poplar, maple (soft), oak, and hickory. I have an infestation of what I assume is powder-post beetles in the maple and poplar joists (many small holes around .5 mm and the creation of a lot of powdery sawdust). The construction is post and beam, so the infested joists can be removed but not without some difficulty. Is there a remedy that can be applied to the surface of the wood that will take care of these critters? Or, is fumigation the only remedy? The house is occupied intermittently on a seasonal basis and has few furnishings.*

From a reader in West Virginia

A The culprit could be powder-post beetles (Lyctidae) or deathwatch beetles (Anobiidae). Both types will attack dry wood. If the frass is the consistency of talcum powder, it is the powder-post beetle. If the frass is coarser than talcum powder but still fine, it is probably deathwatch beetles.

Powder-post beetles have a relatively long life cycle, up to five or more years. Deathwatch beetles have a shorter life cycle. In either case, you have two options. You can treat the wood, if that is possible, with a borate product such as TimBor or Boracare. This will prevent a reinfestation or any new infestations, but it will not kill the larvae that are in the wood. Structural fumigation would kill the larvae but would be relatively expensive. It requires ten times the amount of fumigant necessary for dry-wood termites to control powder-post beetles and four times the amount to kill deathwatch beetles.

I would recommend treating the wood if it is accessible with a borate product.

Q Help!!!

Do I have termites? Every spring (April or May) I come down and find (in the kitchen) about 100 tiny black bugs. There are usually more the second day. With that I set off bug bombs in the kitchen, dining room, and living room.

After that—no more bugs—everything is dead . . . until next year (none upstairs).

My neighbor (we are in attached condos) told me she has termites!! How come mine return every spring? Did my termites leave my house and go to hers? Or are mine still with me? There is no crawl space under our houses. I can't afford a termite exterminator. What should I do? This has been going on for five years.

From a reader in Richmond, VA

A What you describe sounds like swarming termites. Termites swarm every spring to expand to establish new colonies. In some parts of the country they swarm twice a year. Your termites did not go next door. You and your neighbor are probably sharing the same termite colony. I would urge you to get a professional to come over and inspect your home to see if there is any damage in your home. There are companies that offer discounts and have payment plans for folks who can't afford a full payment. If you don't do anything, I am afraid the termites may do damage that will be more costly than the treatment.

3

Biters and Stingers

🕷 This chapter contains the arthropods that occasionally bite and sting humans. A few are obligate parasites of humans while others are only rarely encountered. These are probably the most important of the groups of arthropods that we come in contact with because some of them have the capability of killing people, although deaths by arthropods are rare.

Bed Bugs and Their Relatives

Q *Recently we spent the weekend in our mountain cabin. We were bitten by several small, grayish insects that look like bed bugs. Are there bed bugs in the mountains?*

From a reader in Albuquerque, NM

A You were probably bitten by swallow bugs, which are closely related to bed bugs. Swallow bugs feed on cliff swallows and barn swallows and are common at higher elevations. Their bite is considerably more painful than bed bug bites. You should remove any swallow nests from around the eaves of the cabin. Federal law protects swallows and their nests so this will have to be done before the birds resume nesting next spring. Screening the eaves of the cabin can deter new nesting. Do not use insecticides near the nests, as they are generally highly toxic to the birds.

Q *We think we have bed bugs in one of our bedrooms as we are getting bites at night. How do we know if they are bed bugs and if they are, what should we do?*

From a reader in Las Vegas, NM

A Bed bugs seem to be increasing again as I have received at least ten calls over the past year about this pest. If you are seeing drops of blood on your sheets that is a good indication of bed bugs. Strip the bedding and look carefully along the seams of the mattress for bed bugs and their fecal matter. Also look around the buttons and in any tears in the mattress. Search the box spring as well and then check the bed frame. This is particularly true if the bed frame is wood. Check the places where the bed frame slats fit in the headboard and footboard, as this is a favorite hiding place. Also check behind any pictures or posters on the wall and along the seams of any carpet in the room. If the room has a wooden floor, they may hide between the wood slats.

Bed bugs are about $1/4"$ long, broadly oval in shape, dark brown in color, and almost as flat, before feeding, as a piece of paper. If you find bed bugs you will have to treat all these areas with an insecticide, preferably a synthetic pyrethroid. If you call an exterminator, make sure they do a thorough inspection as outlined above and if they treat, ask them to use a synthetic pyrethroid. They may prefer to use an organophosphate, but they don't have to sleep in the room, you do. Don't hesitate to ask them for references of bed bug jobs they have done in the past, and don't hesitate to call those references to see if they were successful.

Q *We recently had a problem with bed bugs that we successfully exterminated following the advice on a flyer you had written a few years ago. My question is, do bed bugs have any good qualities or are they just bloodsuckers with no redeeming values?*

From a reader in Albuquerque, NM

A I don't know if they have any redeeming qualities, but they are very interesting insects. For instance, they have been used for a number of medicinal purposes. Historically, crushed bed bugs mixed with salt and human milk were considered to be a fine eye ointment. In powdered form they were thought to cure all fevers and for hysteria they were given internally, and just the smell of them was considered sufficient to relieve those suffering from hysterical suffocation. In some parts of

Ohio, eating seven bed bugs mixed with beans is considered a cure for chills and fever.

Bed bugs also have an interesting sex life. The males have large, scimitar-like sex organs with which they pierce the female's body wall, not bothering to use her sex organs. They fill the female's body with semen, some of which makes it to her reproductive organs. The rest is absorbed as protein by the female and used as nourishment. When feeding, bed bugs have been observed climbing on top of another bed bug that is feeding on a human and piercing that bed bug with its beak and sucking the blood from it, thus getting the blood second hand. This body piercing of males by other males and while feeding seems to have no effect on the bed bug getting pierced.

I had a small number of bed bugs I collected a year ago that I kept in captivity for seminars. I fed these bugs on the back of my hand, which worked very well. They survived and reproduced in the cage quite well with a steady diet of my blood. Bed bugs are not known to transmit any diseases so this practice was not dangerous at all and the bites are relatively painless.

Black Widows/Brown Recluse Spiders

Q *How serious a problem is the black widow in the Albuquerque area?*

From a reader in Albuquerque, NM

A There are probably more black widow spiders in Albuquerque than there are people. But the incidence of black widow bites is very low and there have only been a couple deaths in New Mexico that can be attributed to this spider since records have been kept on causes of death. Nationwide there were 1,300 bites and 55 deaths attributed to this spider between 1716 and 1943. By contrast, there are about 1,500 cases of snakebite every year with an average of 75 fatalities. More people die from snakebite every year than have died from black widows in 227 years.

Black widows are very retiring in nature and almost

always try to escape when disturbed. The only time they are even remotely aggressive is if there is an egg case in the web or if they are physically restrained. While they are not aggressive, their bite is extremely venomous and should be considered a major medical emergency.

Here are some tips on keeping black widows and other spiders from making your home their home:

- Maintain tight screening on windows and doors and make sure doors close tightly to keep out spiders' prey.
- Inspect firewood, plants, boxes, or anything else that was stored outside before bringing it in.
- Sweep or vacuum behind washers and dryers regularly as this area is a good place for spiders and their prey because it is dark and moist.
- Move heavy furniture periodically so you can clean beneath it. Keep bedding off the floor.
- Periodically remove and clean curtains, pictures, and other wall decorations.
- Constantly knock down spider webs in the garage before they get a chance to become established.
- In some countries where spiders are a serious problem, it is recommended that you keep the bed at least 8" from the wall to keep wall-crawling spiders out of it.

Q *Wondering if you can help us out with any useful suggestions. We live in Hannibal, Missouri, and I have been reading your column in the* Quincy Herald Whig. *Quincy is 20 miles from us just across the Mississippi River.*

We have had brown recluse spiders invading our house for the past year (or longer??). We hired a well-known exterminating company, and have had little success eliminating the spiders—even after a full year of service. They were using a spray around the baseboards. We have seen the spiders practically every month—often just after they have come to spray. When we complained, they sent someone out to do an extra spraying—at no charge. Wasn't that nice of them? We had to sign a year's contract with them and have been extremely disappointed. If we had known that they couldn't control them, we would have simply done the spraying ourselves. We thought that perhaps they had the answer. We live in an earth-contact house, and do have many bushes close by. They seem to be concentrated in our garage for the most part; however, we have seen them in every room.

Can you help us?

From a reader in Hannibal, MO

A You have a couple of problems judging by your letter. Spraying baseboards cannot control the brown recluse spiders (or any other kind of spider). More on that later. What you should do is to place a large number of glueboards (sticky traps) in areas where the spiders are likely to be found. Place them under and behind furniture and appliances, inside cabinets, in corners, and in the garage. I would suggest you place 50 to 75 glueboards throughout your house. You may want to place some diatomaceous earth or a silica gel under appliances and in the garage. These are dusts that can be applied with a hand-held duster. Keep firewood, bricks, and any other similar material away from your home as this material affords harborage for all sorts of arthropods, including brown recluse spiders.

The second problem is the exterminator you hired. This guy had you sign a contract for a year, sprayed your baseboards for a year, and didn't control anything. He probably thinks he did a good job as he returned when you called to render extra treatments (undoubtedly consisting of spraying the baseboards).

Baseboard spraying was never intended to control pests. When I started in the pest control business over thirty years ago, they told me we were to spray baseboards to kill time in the customer's house. That was the rationale then and it is the rationale now. Baseboard spraying is a gimmick used by pest control operators who do not know what they are doing. It is a generic method used to instill "perceived value" with the customer and will never control any pest. It is practical to spot treat a baseboard occasionally to control silverfish, carpet beetles, or fleas, but it is never necessary to spray baseboards throughout a building. If you see someone spraying baseboards you can rest assured they are poorly trained in the principles of integrated pest management.

What I believe you should do is to contact the pest control company you hired, who gladly took your money without delivering any results, and ask for your money back. If they refuse, I would suggest you take them to court and charge them with malpractice. Incompetence should not be tolerated in the pest control industry and it is not defensible in court.

Bees

Q *Are honeybees the only bees that die after stinging?*
From a reader in Decatur, AL

A Yes, the stingers are barbed and pull loose from the bee causing its death. Unfortunately for the bee, stinging isn't the only way it can kill itself. When a drone (male) inseminates a female, his genitalia are torn loose and remain in the female's vagina serving as a plug to prevent other males from mating with her. The tearing loose of the genitalia is fatal to the male.

Q *How serious is the threat of killer bees?*

Q *How are killer bees controlled?*

Q *Is one killer bee sting fatal and what should I do if they attack me?*

Q *How do I recognize killer bees?*
All from readers in Albuquerque, NM

A To begin with, the term "killer bee" is a bit sensational. Africanized honeybees (AHBs) is a more appropriate name for these insects. Hollywood, the media, and anyone who has a vested interest in scaring the public prefer the term "killer bees." Africanized honeybees are *not* any more aggressive than domestic honeybees, but they are more defensive. They are quicker to defend their colony, they sting in larger numbers, and they will chase an intruder farther, but they do not run around the countryside looking for people to attack.
I do not consider AHBs a serious threat to humans if a few common-sense precautions are taken. Never disturb a

hive of bees for any reason. Never approach a bush or tree with a large number of bees swarming around it and never swat at any bee that gets close to you. If you swat at a bee, she may give off attack/alarm pheromones, which will attract a large number of her colony mates, and you may get seriously stung. The sting of the AHB is no more or less painful or dangerous than the sting from any other honeybee. The venom of the AHB and the domestic bee is almost identical, but AHBs do tend to sting in larger numbers and with less provocation than domestic or European honeybees (EHBs). It is important to remember that if you are allergic to bee venom, any sting can be dangerous, or even fatal.

If any honeybees chase you, cover your head with a jacket or sweater and run to get inside the nearest vehicle, building, or dense vegetation. AHBs have been known to chase people for as much as a quarter of mile, although 100 to 150 yards is a more normal distance to escape attack.

AHBs are generally eradicated when they are found in the wild, but in an apiary there are other alternatives. In an apiary they can be "calmed down" with the introduction of the mellower Italian honeybee queen. When AHBs interbreed with EHBs, the colony tends to get more defensive, but the reverse can also be true by introducing EHBs into an AHB colony. One apiarist has told me that AHBs are actually very good honey producers if they are managed correctly. Apiarists in Central and South America have demonstrated this fact over the years.

The average person cannot recognize an AHB on sight. The bees have to be sent to specialists at the Agricultural Research Service, the U.S. Department of Agriculture's chief research agency, for proper identification. Physically, they look exactly like a domestic (European) honeybee.

Centipedes

Q *Can you suggest a nontoxic way to get rid of house centipedes?*
From a reader in Indianapolis, IN

A House centipedes can usually be controlled by placing glueboards strategically around the house where they are seen, particularly in corners, under furniture, and in damp areas where their prey (silverfish, cockroaches, and crickets) live.

Pesticides are generally not necessary for house centipedes. Be sure to place the glueboards where kids and pets can't get entangled. If you can't find glueboards where you live, you can order them online at *www.callbugaside.com* or by calling 1-866-520-5050. Ask for mouse glueboards, although I would never use them to control mice as I find it extremely inhumane to entrap mice in glueboards.

Q *How many times do you have to hit a centipede with a magazine before it dies?*

From a reader in Placitas, NM

A Lots of times. I recently had a centipede crawl into my bed and bite me on the shoulder when I rolled over on it. Not being rational at 2 A.M., I jumped up and looked around for something to smash it. Finding nothing close by and not wanting to leave, allowing it to escape, I proceeded to slap it silly with my bare hands. The mattress cushioned the blows and after hitting it a couple of dozen times, it was still active and a little annoyed. Had I been able to reach my dresser I would have retrieved my pistol and shot it! Finally I flipped it onto the floor where I easily dispatched it with a shoe. All this time my cat was lying on the floor looking at me like I was some sort of lunatic. Usually when I find centipedes in the house, which has been pretty often this year, I simply scoop them into a jar and place them outside. That is probably what I should have done with the one in my bed. I actually felt bad about killing it the next day.

Q *I have had the most absolutely horrifying and gross-out experience of huge centipedes (6"-plus) in my bed twice in the last month. I have found them in the house, which has been kind of a gross-out, but nothing horrible, particularly since one of cats quickly dispatches them and I usually just find the remains. I have, however, beaten a couple to death with a hammer since just stepping on them doesn't seem to kill them.*

In the first incident, I discovered the centipede when I was making the bed. Scream! Freak out! After that I took care to cover all the drains. (Other websites say they don't come out of the drains, but I know this is B.S. because I have seen them come out of the drains. Once, when rinsing dishes in the sink, a huge one crawled up the drain onto the plate I was rinsing. My neighbor reported that when she was showering one crawled out of the drain up her leg.)

In the second incident the centipede may have come up the shower drain after my boyfriend forgot to cover it after showering the night before. This time it actually crawled on me just as I was dozing off. Before it did, I knew something was weird because my centipede killer kitty who usually has nothing to do with me was up on my pillow batting at something. A few minutes later I felt this weird tickling on my chest. Just as I brushed it away, it tried to sting me but only got a glancing blow, not really a painful sting. It must have been hiding under a large, heavy area rug for a day or so before that because I could see where my kitty had actually dug a hole on one end of the rug trying to get something.

So, what do I do? I know, I know, they are supposed to be beneficial insects, but they are so gross! I'm not a really squeamish person, but I have to tell you that centipedes and cockroaches are the only insects that freak me out. I just went berserk when the centipede crawled on me in my own bed. And before you think I'm an insectist, I carefully move spiders outside when I find them in the house. (I know they're not insects, but you get the drift.) Here's my situation: I live in a 3-year-old custom home that is very tightly constructed. Most of the house is on a slab, but because it is built on a hill, my bedroom is over a crawl space. That part of the house is constructed with tile over gypcrete floors, so I can't imagine the horrible arthropods are squiggling up from the crawl space. What if I have my septic tank pumped and have an exterminator come out and spray it? Is there some sort of repellent I can spray around my bed to sort of create a barrier? I don't like the idea of using strong bug sprays in my bedroom.

Any advice would be greatly appreciated. Thank you very much.

From a reader in Placitas, NM

A That was a very entertaining question. No, don't have the septic tank pumped and sprayed, as that will do nothing except kill some of the beneficial bacteria in the tank. Centipedes certainly can come up drains from septic tanks but I would recommend just keeping the drains closed at night. If you don't have a drain cover for the shower drain, place a zip-lock bag of water on the drain at night. First thing in the morning, run some hot water down the drain to discourage any unwanted guests. Check your doors to make sure they close tightly. If you can see daylight under your doors or if you can slide a piece of paper under the doors then there is enough room for a centipede to come in. If this is the case you may want to install door sweeps on your doors.

I wouldn't recommend spraying any pesticides around your bed. Move your bed away from the wall a few inches. This will prevent centipedes that may climb the wall from getting in the bed. If it is any consolation, you are not alone in having a centipede in bed. Last year I woke up dreaming something was biting me and found a centipede stuck to my shoulder. He crawled in my bed and apparently I rolled over on him triggering a reflex bite on his part (see previous Q and A).

Fleas

Q *Do you recommend flea collars for pets in the Albuquerque area?*
From a reader in Albuquerque, NM

A No, I don't. I picked up one flea collar at the store and the active ingredient was Diazinon, an organophosphate that is a class of insecticides suspected to be carcinogenic. It also said on the box that this flea collar is an "insecticide generator." I don't think I want my cat running around with an "insecticide generator" around her neck.

Some pets have had problems

with flea collars. Symptoms of pesticide overdose in your pet can include vomiting, diarrhea, trembling, seizures, and respiratory problems. Pick up a copy of *The Safe Shopper's Bible* by David Steinman and Samuel S. Epstein, M.D., published by Macmillan. This book cites many brand-name flea collars containing carcinogens, neurotoxins, or both.

It is interesting to note that many insecticide flea and tick shampoos have a warning on the label not to get the product on your skin; however, you are supposed to rub this product into your pet's coat where the skin can absorb it and your pet can lick it.

Fleas are not a major problem where you live, but you can help your pets avoid them with a few practical steps.

- You can add brewer's yeast or nutritional yeast, fresh garlic, or flaxseed oil to pet food for skin health and as a flea repellent.
- Use herb-based flea collars that contain combinations of various herbs that repel fleas, such as lavender, mint, rosemary, sweet woodruff, and cedar.
- Bathe pets with gentle herbal shampoos. Even soap and water will kill fleas if the soap is left on for about five to eight minutes.

These steps are part of a program for battling fleas without toxins that were compiled by People for the Ethical Treatment of Animals (PETA).

I want to make it clear that I am not a doctor of veterinary medicine. I suggest you check with your veterinarian before following the advice in this book or from any other source.

Q *What insect has caused humans more grief than any other?*
From a reader in Chapel Hill, NC

A In my opinion that would be the flea. In 1347, the first cases of the plague, known as the Black Death, appeared in Europe, and the disease was well established by 1348. The plague was so infectious that whole towns ceased to exist and fleeing people spread the plague far and wide. Before the end of the outbreak, about a third of the population of Europe was dead; this is the highest percentage of a population ever killed by an epidemic. The Black Death was so effective that there were not enough people left in many areas to bury the dead.

In 1664 and 1665, the plague returned to London, killing 100,000 people. It struck again in China in 1892, spread throughout southern Asia and ended by killing 6 million people in India.

These plague-carrying fleas have caused more grief than any other force in history. The combined efforts of Nero and Genghis Khan, of Napoleon and Adolf Hitler, of Idi Amin and Saddam Hussein, and of Pol Pot and Joseph Stalin pale in comparison to the flea's ravages throughout the ages. By the way, does anyone notice that when you compile of list of lunatics, despots, megalomaniacs, and other assorted folks with bad habits, there are rarely any women on the list? Maybe the world is being run by the wrong sex.

Lice

Q *My child came home from school infested with lice. What should we do?*

From a reader in Oklahoma

A Lice seem to be resurging after a long period of very few cases. There is some evidence they are becoming resistant to commercial pesticides. A friend and colleague, Dr. Jenella Loye, has done extensive research on this problem and these are her recommendations:

The safest, most effective control is grooming. A nightly comb-out with coconut oil or hair conditioner can control infestations. The best combs are those designed and manufactured in Old World countries such as India, Pakistan, the Middle East, and Southeast Asia. Some of the common brands of combs are inferior for removing nits.

Over-the-counter shampoos contain pyrethroid pesticides, which have been used for pest control for many years. If you use them, use them carefully and keep in mind that many lice are becoming resistant to commercial insecticide shampoos. Treat only the area (the head) infested with lice. Do not apply in the shower as warm skin takes up toxins into the blood stream more readily. Read the label carefully and do not leave on the head any longer than is recommended.

Remember that all testing for toxicology occurs on adult white males so reactions in other people may vary. Children and the elderly are particularly susceptible to toxic overload. Prescription shampoos contain lindane, a chlorinated hydrocarbon similar to chlordane, which was once used to control termites. The use of lindane on humans is controversial because it is extremely toxic and is thought to be carcinogenic.

Q *I found this bug on my head and think it is a louse. Is it, and if so, what should I do?*

From a reader in Albuquerque, NM

A The insect you brought in is a louse, but not a species that normally lives on the head. The solution is simple. Shave the infested areas. Lice spend their lives hanging on to body hairs. Also, boil all underwear and linens to kill any lice that became dislodged from the body.

This louse, known as the pubic louse, spends its entire life about 1/2" from where it hatched from an egg. They do not spread over the entire body very well. A pubic louse can only move at the rate of 4" a day! Its slender cousin, the head louse can race along at 7" per hour and is quite capable of visiting various parts of the body.

Do not use the mercuric ointment that has been around forever. It is neither effective nor safe. Its value as an insecticide is low, and it carries the potential of causing serious poisoning.

Scorpions

Q *I think my leg is being pulled, but just in case, will go ahead and ask the questions: Do scorpions have some sort of glow-in-the-dark power, presumably to attract bugs to them that they then eat? And, have scorpions survived atomic blasts? (I'm told they were found at ground zero after the White Sands test.)*

From a reader in Placitas, NM

A These are good questions. Scorpions do fluoresce under ultraviolet light but the reason for this ability is not clear. Scorpionologists have theorized that this ability serves as an ultraviolet-sensitivity mechanism. Some have suggested it is used to attract insects to be used as food. I doubt if that is the purpose for a couple of reasons. First, scorpions glow under ultraviolet light even after death, and second, other organisms that are not predators also fluoresce. There are some species of fluorescent sow bugs in California, a couple of species of millipedes, and some species of moths that glow in the pupal stage. None of these arthropods would want to attract insects. One very beneficial purpose of the scorpion's glow is it makes them easy to find. We can walk through the desert at night carrying a black light (ULV light) and easily detect the glowing scorpions, which can then be collected. The downside is that rattlesnakes don't glow in the dark, so you have to be careful when hunting scorpions.

As for the second part of your question, scorpions along with a number of other arthropods, seem to do well after atomic blasts. I do not know of any studies at White Sands, but there have been a number of ecological studies completed at the Nevada test sites and a number of arthropods, including scorpions, were collected after testing.

Q *I am hoping you can help. In the past 24 hours, we have discovered two scorpions in our home (in Albuquerque). The sight of these creatures both startled and frightened me, and after doing research, I am further horrified by the findings.*

The scorpions were both about $1^1/2$" to 2" in length, yellowish brown in color with pinchers, tail barb, and eight legs. Definitely

true scorpions and possibly (to my dread) the Centruroides sculpturatus. *The first was found last night around 10 P.M. in the hall-
way of our second story. The second, discovered this evening around
5, was clinging to a damp towel waiting to go into the washer. This
was close to the back door.*

*We have two small children, one three years old and the other
almost ten months. There are toys, blankets, etc., scattered around
the house on the floor. We spend most of our days sitting around
on the floor playing. Now, I am sitting at the computer with my
feet up on the chair. I am worried that the scorpions could be everywhere! Paranoid, I know, but still, I am forcing my husband to
check the kids every half hour!!*

*What are the chances that these creatures are actually the
bark scorpions? Do they live in groups? Should I expect to see more
and more? I have no black light, so is there another safe way to
check for companions? What can I do to rid the house of scorpions since I heard that pesticides don't work?*

*Sorry to bombard you with questions, but I do hope you can
help. It is late at night, and I have no idea who else can answer.
Please contact me as soon as possible to assist with ending our pest
problem. I really appreciate any feedback you can offer. Thank
you, in advance, from a true scorpio-phobe!*

From a reader in Albuquerque, NM

A You do not have the bark scorpion, *Centruroides exilicauda
(C. sculpturatus* has been suppressed for nomenclatural reasons), because it doesn't live in this area. In New Mexico, the
bark scorpion is restricted to Hidalgo, Grant, Catron, and
southern McKinley counties. In this area we have three
species, none of which are dangerous. They are the Coahuila
scorpion, *(Vaejovis coahuilae),* Russell's scorpion *(Vaejovis
russelli),* and the sand scorpion *(Paruroctonus utahensis).* The
Coahuila scorpion is the most common and is found all
around Albuquerque. Russell's scorpion is not common and
it appears to be restricted to the West Side, and the sand
scorpion is common in sandy habitats. I have been stung by
all three species with no serious consequences. Even the
bark scorpion that has caused fatalities in Arizona and
Mexico has never killed anyone in New Mexico. One leading scorpionologist told me there may be clinal variations

in the venom within species, meaning the venom could be lethal in some areas and not in others.

As for your house, the best thing you can do is remove any ground litter, firewood, bark mulch, and similar hiding places. Also make sure your doors close tightly even if it means installing drag strips on the doors. Scorpions are solitary animals, so you may or may not see others, but the individuals you do see can be killed with a shoe, fly swatter, or a rolled-up newspaper. Pesticides are not necessary for scorpion control. Because you have two small children, I would not recommend pesticides under any circumstances either in or around your home.

Ticks

Q We are new to the Southwest and my husband likes to hunt. Back east we were concerned about deer ticks and Lyme Disease. Is that a concern here and should he take any precautions when hunting to prevent ticks?

From a reader in Moriarty, NM

A Lyme Disease is carried by two species of "deer" ticks: the Eastern black-legged tick *(Ixodes scapularis)* and the Western black-legged tick *(Ixodes pacificus)*. Neither species is found in New Mexico, although they are found in surrounding states. We have three other species of deer ticks, but they are not known carriers of Lyme Disease. Your husband and other hunters should take normal precautions because other ticks are present and will bite. They should wear long-sleeved shirts and have their pants tucked into their boots in areas of heavy brush.

Q I am starting to find ticks on my dog. Is there any nontoxic method for controlling ticks outdoors and indoors if they get in the house?

From a reader in the Isleta Pueblo, NM

A You probably found the brown dog tick. This tick rarely bites humans but it can cause various diseases in dogs. These very prolific ticks mate on a dog, then fall off and lay from 1,000 to 5,000 eggs in cracks and crevices. Eggs hatch in $2^1/2$ weeks to two months. The larval stage (or seed tick) attaches itself to a host and feeds for three to six days, then falls off and molts into a nymph. This stage lasts about a month before the tick reaches adulthood. Adult brown dog ticks can live over 500 days without a blood meal.

Here are some suggestions:

- Inspect your free-roaming pets regularly for ticks. Search particularly around the ears and toes.
- Remove embedded ticks with tweezers by pulling gently without twisting. Be careful not to break off the tick's mouthparts that are embedded in the animal.
- Clean wounds made by ticks with soap and water, and then apply an antiseptic.
- Comb or remove ticks elsewhere on the pet's body.
- Indoors, designate specific sleeping areas for dogs to reduce the size of the dog-tick infestation.
- Vacuum and use sorptive dusts (diatomaceous earth or silica gel) in cracks, then caulk the cracks.
- Outdoors, use a tick drag or carbon dioxide trap to locate the ticks and reduce their numbers.
- Keep vegetation cut below ankle level to reduce tick harborage.
- Remove woodpiles and other areas where mice may live and keep bird feeders away from the house.

A tick drag is a 4' by 6' piece of white flannel attached to a stick. You drag the flannel through the yard. Any ticks in the vegetation will attach themselves to the flannel where they can be seen and destroyed.

A carbon dioxide trap is simply a covered ice bucket or Styrofoam container with several holes in the sides near the bottom. Place two pounds of dry ice in the bucket and place the bucket on a piece of white flannel or a piece of plywood with a masking-tape barrier. The tape should be stapled to the plywood sticky side up. The dry ice should last about three hours and attract every tick within a 75-square-foot area around the trap.

Wasps/Yellow Jackets

Q We found something in our yard that a neighbor called a velvet ant. What is a velvet ant?

From a reader in Rio Rancho, NM

A Velvet ants are not really ants, but are wasps. They are usually brightly colored, black with red, orange or white, or some species are all white. The wingless females wander around looking for ground-dwelling bees and wasps to parasitize.

When the females are disturbed, they produce an acoustical warning (squeaking noise) that reinforces their bright warning coloration. If handled, velvet ants (also known as cow killers and mule killers) can deliver an attention-getting sting. I have been bitten and stung by almost everything that bites and stings—including venomous snakes, black widows, scorpions, centipedes, assassin bugs, wheel bugs, bed bugs, and countless ants, bees, and wasps—and the sting of a velvet ant in my opinion ranks with the best of them in pain. I no longer walk barefoot in my yard. On the other hand, I would never kill them either as they have a place in nature, as does everything else.

Q Hornets are coming to the outdoor lights on our deck and our upstairs balcony at night. They are over an inch in length, with yellow/brown large bodies, and are mean. I don't see them during the day—but we cannot go out on our deck or balcony at night with the light on. . . . We cannot find a nest (and really don't know what to look for). This has been going on for at least 6 weeks. I turned on my overhead light in the bedroom upstairs tonight and they came to the screen door at the balcony and were trying to get in. That's when my husband said, "Please write the Bugman. . . ." So help, again, and thanks!

From a reader in Richmond, VA

A There is good news about your hornets. They are European hornets, and they differ from our domestic species in that they fly at night (as you know). The good news is that they are not trying to get in, they are simply attracted to the household lights. They are not aggressive and they feed on a wide variety of insects that are pests including large grasshoppers, horse flies, house flies, bees, and yellow jackets. They are often drawn to lighted windows causing unwarranted alarm to the people inside, and it seems like this is exactly what is happening at your place. They feed the insects mentioned above to their young. The adult hornets feed on sap and will girdle some plants to get to the sap.

As a rule, these are very beneficial insects. They would be hard to control if that is what you wanted to do, as it would be very hard to find the colony. Sorry I can't be of more help.

Q *I have yellow jackets around my house but I can't find the nest. I don't know when they return to their nests, so I can't follow them. How can I locate their nests?*

From a reader in Tucson, AZ

A Yellow jackets generally nest in the ground but occasionally will nest in hollow logs, cinder block fences, and other areas with voids. One way to get the yellow jackets to return to their nests when you want them to is to dust them with flour. Puff some flour on a foraging yellow jacket and it will automatically (in most cases) head right back to its nest. All you have to do is follow it, then go out at night and destroy the nest or hire a professional to destroy it for you.

Q *We have a lot of wasps and yellow jackets on our property every year. What can you tell us that will help us get along with them without killing them?*

From a reader in Albuquerque, NM

A Here are a few helpful hints you can use to live in peace with the bees, wasps, and yellow jackets on your property.

- Never work in the yard or garden wearing yellow or white. These colors attract insects. If you wear perfume or cologne in addition to yellow, you may be mistaken for a big flower. Many insects cannot see red, making it a good color to wear when working in your yard.

- If you have a backyard cookout, you may want to set out some baited yellow jacket traps at the far end of the yard. It is also a good idea to set out a yellow plastic tub of water with a couple of drops of dish soap in it. The insects will be attracted to the yellow tub and when they hit the water they will sink because the soap eliminates the surface tension that would normally allow them to float.
- Always put pet food and water in dark bowls, preferably red. Yellow food bowls will attract these insects.

Here are some tips if a bee, wasp, or yellow jacket stings you:

- If you are not sure which kind of insect stung you, examine the wound for the presence of a stinger. Bees have a barbed stinger that is left in the wound (thereby killing the bee). Wasps and yellow jackets can sting repeatedly, leaving no stinger behind.
- Wash the wound immediately. I usually follow washing by applying meat tenderizer that has been made into a paste by adding a little water. Meat tenderizer contains enzymes that destroy the proteins in the venom. There are also commercially available products that reduce the pain from stings.
- Rest and don't drink alcohol. If the sting is on a limb and it swells, lower it below your body trunk. If the sting is on the mouth or throat, seek immediate medical attention, as swelling in these areas could cause suffocation.
- If the sting is followed by severe symptoms, you may be hypersensitive to bee and wasp venom. In this situation, the sting should be considered a major medical emergency and the victim should be rushed to a hospital. Signs of hypersensitivity include itching, flushing, hives, and swelling distant from the sting site. Other reactions include hypotension (low blood pressure) with dizziness, unconsciousness, cyanosis (blueness), nausea, vomiting, chest pains, abdominal

or pelvic cramps, and headache. These symptoms begin anywhere from a few seconds to 30 minutes after a sting and can last for several hours.

- If you know you are hypersensitive to bee and wasp stings, you should have in your possession several preloaded epinephrine injectors as part of your first aid kit and you should carry the kit when you are in areas where you may encounter bees, wasps, or yellow jackets.

Wheel Bugs

Q *I was recently bitten by a large bug that looked like a dinosaur. It had a hood on its neck and the bite was very painful. The doctor asked me to get it identified because of the severity of the symptoms from the bite. Do you know what it is based on my description?*

From a reader in Albuquerque, NM

A You were bitten by a wheel bug *(Arilus cristatus)*. It is a large bug, more than an inch long with a semicircular ridge rising behind the head. The ridge has 8 to 12 uniformly arranged teeth resembling short spikes or cogs on a wheel.

The wheel bug is in the assassin bug family and they feed on insects, particularly caterpillars, and because of their size, they can handle relatively large prey. Wheel bugs are not common and few people are bitten, but I can tell you from experience that the bite will get your attention. I was bitten on the finger several years ago and the intense pain lasted for hours and there was a dull throbbing around the bite that persisted for several weeks.

Wheel bugs are beneficial insects and they should never be killed, nor should they be handled.

4

Odds and Ends

🐜 This chapter contains questions and answers on unusual or regional pests that occasionally plague homeowners. None can be considered major destructive or dangerous pests, but they can be a nuisance.

Aphids

Q *How can I get rid of aphids on my houseplants without spraying chemicals?*

From a reader in Vero Beach, FL

A If the plant is small enough to hold in your hand, you can dip it in a mixture of soap and water. Use any container large enough to dip the plant without breaking off its stems. The bathtub, a large shallow pan, or something similar will do. Fill the container with warm water and add liquid dish soap at a ratio of 2 tablespoons to 1 gallon of water. Turn the plant upside down, while securing the soil with a towel, plastic, newspapers, or aluminum foil, and swish the plant around in the water. After dislodging the aphids or other bugs, you can rinse the plant off in cold water. Use your fingers to rub the leaves to dislodge any insects that may not have come off in the bath. This treatment will work on aphids, thrips, scales, and spider mites.

Soaking a couple of cigarettes in water for a couple of days and then adding the nicotine water to the bath water can make a stronger dip liquid. For spider mites, you can mix 2 cups of buttermilk into a gallon of water, dip the plant, and let the solution remain on the leaves overnight before rinsing it off.

One word of caution: Never dip cacti, African violets, or any plants with hairy leaves or stems.

Asian Ladybird Beetles

Q *We are having a terrible time with ladybugs in our house. Do you have any suggestions for getting rid of them without using pesticides?*

From a reader in Richmond, VA

A The lady bugs you have are Asian ladybird beetles. They were introduced into this country by the U.S. Department of Agriculture to help control aphids. Unfortunately, they have the disconcerting habit of overwintering in homes. They enter houses through very small openings and seek out dark, quiet areas such as attics, crawl spaces, wall voids, and similar places. On warm winter days they may become active and be noticeable throughout the home.

The best method of control is to vacuum them up. You can put some diatomaceous earth in the vacuum cleaner bag to kill the insects. Make sure you empty the bag after using it so you don't get the distinctive odor of dead ladybugs.

You will also want to closely inspect the outside of your home and seal, caulk, or screen any opening small enough to admit these beetles.

Booklice

Q *I recently bought some old books at a used bookstore and when I opened one of them some small bugs fell out. Can you tell me what they are and what to do about them?*

From a reader in Ventnor, NJ

A The bugs you sent to me are booklice. Booklice are small, grayish, soft-bodied insects that superficially resemble head lice. They primarily feed on molds and can damage books when they eat the starch sizing in the bindings. There are a number of species of booklice but only a few interact with people. One species is known to feed on the pollen in beehives.

Placing a book in a microwave oven for 30 to 60 seconds can kill booklice. Studies completed at State University of New York at Syracuse have determined that most books can undergo this treatment without any damage. The glue on paperbacks may soften initially, causing the book to curl a little, but it will soon flatten out if placed on a flat surface. Placing very old books made of parchment or other fragile paper in a microwave is not recommended because the paint in color illustrations contains metallic salts—microwaves and metals don't mix.

Box-Elder/Red-Shouldered Bugs

Q *We have some little black beetle-like bugs all over our house. Can you tell us what they are and how to get rid of them?*
From a reader in Albuquerque, NM

Q *Box-elder bugs have taken over our home. Last summer was the first time we had problems with them. As cold weather arrived they moved into the house (I killed 60 in one day). Now that spring is here they have returned outside. I called a pest control service and was told spraying won't help. What can you suggest? My neighbors aren't bothered by them. We don't have any box-elder trees, so where do they come from? Any information would be appreciated.*

From a reader in Michigan

A The bugs that were brought in by the reader in Albuquerque are red-shouldered bugs. They are very common around homes and commercial buildings that have golden rain, box-elder, or soapberry trees planted nearby. They are quite common on campus near these trees. Red-shouldered bugs are entirely harmless and pose no health threat to anyone, but they are a nuisance. In your home you should just vacuum them up. You also need to make sure your home is tightly sealed to prevent these little insects from entering. Doors should close tightly and all screens should be in good repair. These bugs are resistant to insecticides but can be killed if directly sprayed with soap and water. The other alternative is removing the tree that is the source of the infestation.

The box-elder bugs plaguing the reader from Michigan can also be infesting maple trees as well as box-elder trees.

Box-elder bugs can be controlled using the same methods used for red-shouldered bugs.

Conifer Seed-Eating Bugs

Q *Our house is infested with large bugs that just sit on the wall and don't appear to move. They don't seem to do any damage but it is disconcerting to have them around. Can you tell me what they are and what to do about them?*

From a reader in Tijeras Canyon, NM

A The bugs you sent at my request are conifer seed-eating bugs, also known as leaf-footed bugs. They are closely related to squash bugs. Conifer seed-eating bugs feed on the seeds of a variety of conifers, including pine. These bugs often migrate into homes in the fall to overwinter. Although they do not occur in large congregations, their large size and appearance can cause alarm. They do have a slight odor but they do not bite nor can they reproduce indoors. Sealing the home in late summer is the best way to prevent these bugs from reoccurring next year. The bugs already in your home can simply be picked up and placed outside or vacuumed up. Chemicals are not necessary for controlling conifer seed-eating bugs.

Earwigs

Q *We have been plagued by earwigs for the past three or four years. Ours is a farming-suburban community; outbuildings, mailboxes, bird houses (1" to 2" deep); garden crops such as lettuce, parsley, basil, sage destroyed; roses, peonies, clematis chewed beyond recognition;* and *inside our homes (open a door and they fall everywhere)! What can be done to control these pests?*

From a reader in Richmond, VA

A Earwigs are small, brown insects with a pair of forcep-like appendages in the rear. They live in moist habitats and are omnivorous, which means they feed on animal and plant material. Some species are pests in the garden as the second writer has suggested. You need to modify the habitat around your home if possible by moving any firewood, boards, or other debris away from the house. If you have a lot of rocks (western landscaping) then all you can do is prevent them from entering your home. Make sure your doors and windows are tight fitting and that the screens are in good repair. Earwigs already in the home can be vacuumed up. Put some diatomaceous earth in the vacuum cleaner bag to kill the earwigs (and any other insects or spiders you vacuum up). Earwigs cannot breed indoors and they do not crawl in people's ears and drive them insane as an ancient English superstition claims.

As for the plants, you can apply a cover of diatomaceous earth around the plants they are feeding on. You can also roll up wet newspapers and put them in the garden. The earwigs will feed at night and hide in the newspaper during the day where you can find and destroy them.

Elm Leaf Beetles

Q *We are having a large number of small greenish beetles all over the house. We just moved here this summer. Is this normal? Did we bring them in with the firewood? Should we get the house sprayed?*

From a reader in Albuquerque, NM

A If you live near some elm trees this is normal. You didn't bring them in with firewood and you don't need your house sprayed. These little insects are elm leaf beetles and they generally enter homes, garages, sheds, and other shelters in the late fall or early winter. They will hide in any place available and often in enormous numbers. It is too late to keep them out this year, but you want to try to seal your home as much as possible to prevent them next year. Make sure your screens are tight fitting and your windows and doors close tightly. If you have any vents on the outside of the house, cover them with fine mesh.

Elm leaf beetles do no damage indoors and do not bite, but they are a nuisance because they get into everything. The beetles that are now in your home can be vacuumed up. If they are scattered throughout the home you may want to use an ultraviolet light at night to attract them to one area where they can then be vacuumed up. Put a couple of mothballs in the vacuum cleaner bag to kill the beetles.

Plaster Beetles

Q *One of my customers in Santa Fe has built a straw-bale home and now he is infested with very small beetles. What are the beetles and how do I get rid of them for my customer?*
From a pest control operator in Santa Fe, NM

A The beetles you asked me to identify are plaster beetles (family Lathridiidae), also known as minute brown scavenger beetles. These very small beetles (1 to 3 mm in length) feed on molds and can become a nuisance in this kind of construction, because straw-bale homes often have mold in the straw. The beetles can live and breed in the straw walls, developing into very large numbers and eventually emerging all over the house. There is no practical treatment for this problem at the present time, short of structurally fumigating the house. This, however, is very expensive and would not prevent the beetles from reinfesting as long as mold is still present. Plaster beetles are also occasionally found in conventional homes if there is a plumbing leak in the home. They will feed on any mold that develops from the leak.

The name "plaster beetle" is not indicative of a single species of beetle. There are a number of species of beetles in this family and they all have the same general habits. In the outdoors they live under the bark of dead stumps and logs feeding on molds. Any of the species could be found in homes although several forms are rare and have restricted distributional ranges and will probably not turn up in a house.

Roly-Polys

Q *I am looking for some help. My cucumber plant is dying and I think the culprit is roly-poly bugs. Right at the base of the stem is an area that has been damaged and there are many of these bugs in close proximity.*

From a reader in North Carolina

A Pillbugs (roly-polys) and the closely related sow bugs are not insects, but are the only crustaceans that have adapted to life on land. Sow bugs are unable to roll up into a ball as the pillbugs do. These interesting creatures were introduced into North America and now thrive in yards all over the country. Although adapted to land, pillbugs and sow bugs seek out moist locations and cannot survive for long in dry areas.

When growing susceptible plants, avoid the use of organic mulches that provide shelter for pillbugs. Coarse mulches may be used if the site dries rapidly, and black plastic mulches on beds that receive a lot of sunlight in summer, which is unfavorable to pillbugs. Barriers of diatomaceous earth will also repel pillbugs and there is a bait available for them also.

Snails

Q *First, thank you for a really useful, comfortable column. I garden and teach middle school, but I'm still bug phobic. Thanks to you, however, my little can of Raid is still half full.*

Second, although I really appreciate your "balance-of-nature" point of view, I do not see any redeeming features in snails. My cats play in the garden, so I use diatomaceous earth, but give me a cool, rainy morning, and I will stomp 20 to 25 snails on my walk through the neighborhood. I guess I'm not likely to wipe out the snail population, but I can change my "hobby" if you can convince me snails do anything but chomp down my tomato plants. Clarify this please?

From a reader in Albuquerque, NM

A I probably can't list too many redeeming qualities of snails. In fact, I can't think of any. However, I would like to see you change your "hobby" for one reason, and that is there is no good reason to stomp every snail you see, especially if it is no threat to your plants. We have snails on campus and they are pests and we use a variety of ways to control them including diatomaceous earth, trapping, and, in some cases, baits. But when I see them after a rain crawling across the sidewalk I pick them up and put them out of harm's way. I can't bring myself to stomp something just because it is in my way. Like everything else, they have a place in nature although that place may not be evident to us. Please don't stomp on the snails.

Q *Every year we get a lot of snails in our yard and I imagine we will get them this year. Is there anything we can do to control them? Are there any pesticides that work on snails?*

From a reader in St. Louis, MO

A Yes to both questions, although I don't recommend pesticides for snails. Most snail baits contain metaldehyde as the active ingredient. Not only is there evidence that snails are becoming resistant to it, but to make matters worse, the bait is often extremely attractive to dogs. Metaldehyde can cause convulsions in a dog and often will kill it.

There are several traps you can make for snails. One simple trap consists of a piece of plywood about 12" square on 1" risers. The snails will gather under the board and can be collected every morning and be disposed of. You can also mix a little stale beer with some wheat flour and place this mixture in Mason jar lids and set them in your garden. You can collect the inebriated snails the next morning. Other attractants that will bring snails out where they can be collected are raw slices of turnips or potatoes.

Q *I am curious as to how snails manage to stay so plentiful. I know they are hermaphrodites, but if you kill all of the ones in the*

*garden, where do the new ones come from? Where are they lurk-
ing and what is their status?*

Thanks so much.

From a reader in Albuquerque, NM

A That is a good question and you are right about their her-
maphroditism. Each animal has both male and female sex
organs. Cross-fertilization is most common but cases of self-
fertilization have been reported. Individual snails may lay up
to 100 eggs, depending on the species, but usually the number is smaller. The brown garden snail lays egg masses an
inch in diameter that contains an average of 86 eggs.

Young snails remain in the nest for several days and do
not wander far from the area for several months. This is
important to know when controlling snails since a large
number of young snails in one area is a clue to where they
are laying eggs.

Snails require a damp environment and fairly humid air
to survive. They hide under boards and rocks in shady areas
along with damp leaves and other moist materials. They
return to the same place every night using the same route
each time unless their usual resting-place dries out. If the air
or the substrate becomes too dry, a snail can pull its entire
body into the shell and seal the opening with a sheet of
mucous, which then hardens, forming a secure closure. It can
remain dormant in this condition for as long as four years.

As you can see, they are pretty resilient little animals.

Squash Bugs

Q *Do you have any suggestions for control of squash bugs on pump-
kins? Hand-picking doesn't seem to keep up with them this year.
I'd love an organic solution if there is one, but if not, chemical
will do.*

From a reader in Oklahoma

A You can try putting newspaper, boards, or other sources of
shelter near the plants where the bugs will congregate when
they are not feeding so that they can be collected and

destroyed. It is also easy to spot their egg masses on the undersides of leaves (they look like small ball bearings). They can be crushed when found. If you decide to use chemicals, spray the plants when the egg masses are found with permethrin, carbaryl, or sabadilla, followed by a second treatment approximately 2 weeks later. Diatomaceous earth applied around the base of the plant is also effective.

Sun Spiders

Q *I had this long, tan bug with long legs, black fangs, and long antennae in my house. My neighbor said it was a child-of-the-earth and a relative said it was a sun spider and I should get my house sprayed. Can you tell what it is by my description or should I bring it in?*

From a reader in Albuquerque, NM

A You saw a sun spider, also known as a wind scorpion or solpugid. They are really not spiders but they are arachnids and are related to spiders and scorpions. Sun spiders are yellowish-brown and larger than most spiders. They are very common in our area but are usually active at night and are rarely seen. They hide under rocks and debris during the day. Sun spiders occasionally enter homes in search of insect prey and although they look intimidating, they are harmless. They will bite, however, if you pick them up and the bite can be painful.

You can discourage sun spiders in your home by keeping harborage areas away from the foundation (rocks, firewood, ground debris, etc.). Make sure your doors close tightly as they will often come in this way.

Sweat Bees

Q *What are those little bees that pester me when I am mowing my lawn? At least I think they are bees. They look like baby honeybees.*

From a reader in Belen, NM

A The bees you are referring to are sweat bees. These small bees range in size from 3 to 5 mm, with a few species reaching $1/2$" in length.

They are mostly black, with light-colored transverse abdominal stripes, but some are metallic brass or copper colored, or iridescent green or blue.

Sweat bees are attracted to human sweat and they can be a nuisance. These bees nest in the ground in tunnels that are deposited with pollen and nectar for the young. Although they are not social insects, sweat bees will often share a tunnel. It's just a method of conserving energy and affords additional protection against parasitism by other insects.

Sweat bees sometimes sting when brushed away while drinking perspiration from a person's body. The sting is very mild, and the effects last only a few minutes.

If you are bothered by sweat bees, flick them away with a finger rather than brushing them. It is not possible to control sweat bees, nor is it necessary.

Tiger Beetles

Q *I have seen this really cool beetle-type bug that runs really fast, at night, with an wildly iridescent carapace. Do you know what it is? It is about 1" long and seems to have a white splotch near its head. I love 'em.*

Dick, you've made me into such a bug lover. I actually catch the German cockroaches and take them outside. They are such a lovely gold I can't bear to kill them.

From a reader in Las Cruces, NM

A The beetle you are seeing running around is a tiger beetle. There are a number of species of this beautiful beetle and some of them are quite rare. They should never be killed.

Tiger beetles are predaceous on other insects, sometimes pouncing on them quite suddenly. They run and fly close to the ground quite rapidly. Usually they are found in open sunny areas and can sometimes be found in good numbers. The larvae construct vertical burrows in hard-packed ground and wait at the top of the burrow for unsuspecting prey.

Tiger beetles are easily recognized by their large eyes, black or brown color with light markings. Most are iridescent blue or green below and are $1/2$" to 1" in length.

As for the German cockroach release program you developed, all I can say is congratulations! Why kill something just because it is a temporary nuisance? Placing them outside is much better than spraying pesticides all over the place.

Vinegaroons

Q *I saw this very large, black, scorpion-looking animal in my garage. It had huge pincers and a long stinger. What is it and how do I keep them away from my house?*

From a reader in Albuquerque, NM

A What you saw was a completely harmless, but intimidating-looking vinegaroon. Vinegaroons may reach a length of $3^1/2$". They are distant relatives to the scorpion but they are unable to sting you. The long "stinger" at the end of their body is actually used to spray a chemical when they are threatened. The large claws are used to catch prey such as crickets, cockroaches, and other arthropods. The long feeler-like legs are used to help them find their way around, as they are very nearsighted.

Vinegaroons are active at night and hide during the day under rocks, leaves or other ground litter. They have a curious mating ritual that looks like two front loaders doing a square dance. After mating the female hides in a shelter and lays from 7 to 35 large eggs. She stays with the eggs attached to her body until they have hatched and undergone several molts. After the young move on with their lives, the female dies.

Vinegaroons are very interesting animals and they are completely harmless. All you have to do is gently pick them up and place them outside. If that takes a little more courage than is available, then you can push one onto a dustpan or piece of cardboard to carry it outside. Vinegaroons should never be killed.

Whiteflies

Q *Any suggestions on controlling whiteflies?*

From a reader in Corrales, NM

A Whiteflies are not true flies. They are more closely related to aphids, scales, and mealybugs.

Adult female whiteflies deposit 200 to 400 eggs in circular clusters on the underside of leaves. The eggs hatch in five to ten days into nymphs, which go through several stages before they pupate. It takes about 25 days for the eggs to hatch and the nymphs to reach adulthood. New hatched whiteflies resemble small mealybugs.

After three or four days they settle down on a plant and molt, losing their legs in the process. For the next three molts they remain attached to the plant like a scale insect. When the adults emerge, they breed and start the cycle over.

The adults are small, about one/sixteenth of an inch long and have white, powdery wings. Whiteflies can cause wilting, chlorosis, loss of leaves or stunting if they are present in high numbers. In addition, whiteflies produce a honeydew secretion that in turn may produce a black fungus known as sooty mold. Sooty mold does not damage the leaf but will make the plant look dirty.

Usually people are more upset because of the little adult whiteflies flying around. You can make a whitefly trap by cutting quarter-inch plywood, masonite or cardboard into rectangular pieces approximately one foot by two feet and painting both sides with Rustoleum yellow No. 659. When the paint is dry you can then cover the board with a sticky adhesive. This shade of yellow has been shown in tests to be particularly attractive to whiteflies.

Drill holes and hang the board over the plants. Solvents are needed to remove the whiteflies and fungus gnats that will get caught. The solvents will remove the sticky adhesive as well, so it will have to be replaced before the board can be reused.

In greenhouses, a parasitoid known as *Encarsia formosa* does a very good job of controlling whiteflies. This little wasp is available from biological supply houses.

5

Rodents, Reptiles, and Other Nonbugs

🐜 This section deals with the nonbugs, or vertebrates that occasionally interact with people. Most are harmless but some can cause concern, and in the case of deer mice, can be a serious health hazard.

Gophers

Q Help!! *I have been plagued for years by these ever-present creatures, but this year has been the worst. My garden looks like a battlefield and I do not know what to try next. Have done flares, traps, flooding, mothballs, etc. Do you know of anything I can use/do (apart from cannons which I know will disturb the neighbors!) to keep them from devouring and demolishing my garden completely?*

From a reader in Lodi, CA

A When I had gophers several years ago, I planted another garden in the far end of my yard for them, giving them veggies I don't like. Once they became established in their own garden, I replanted mine and had no further trouble from them. This worked for two years, after which the gophers moved on by themselves.

Another method of gopher control that works fairly well is using a repellent. There is a product called Gopher-Med Repellent available from Gardens Alive! You spray it on the ground and it soaks in and repels gophers for up to 2 months, although in some situations you may have to reapply it more often. (Information on Gardens Alive! is available in the chapter on Resources.)

Finally, a reader wrote to me and told me he controlled

his gophers by pouring garlic salt into their burrows. He didn't say how much to pour in or why it worked. You can take this bit of advice with a "grain of salt."

Mice and Rats

Q *What is the best way to get rid of mice?*
From a reader in Albuquerque, NM

A I prefer to use live traps such as Tin Cats on campus. I bait these traps with oatmeal and then release the mice. Each trap will hold several mice. If you prefer, snap traps are still the mainstays in mouse control. I use them as a last resort or if I suspect the mouse is a deer mouse. The best baits for snap traps are Tootsie Rolls, Slim Jims, or gumdrops. These snacks stick to the mouse's teeth and they can't lick them off the trap like peanut butter and they don't dry out like cheese. I never use rodent poisons on campus and I never recommend them. Mice that take the poison may die in an inconvenient place and cause an odor for a few days. This could be hazardous if the mouse is a deer mouse. The stories that mice go outside to look for water and then die or that the poison mummifies them somehow so they don't smell are both wrong. Mice usually die in some hidden area, often where you may not be able to reach them. If your extermina-  tor uses mouse poisons, ask him if his service includes coming back, locating the carcass, and removing it. If your exterminator does not provide this service, you may want to insist on traps. Glueboards also work but they are unnecessarily cruel and I never use them for that reason. Pest control doesn't have to be barbaric to be successful.

Q *We recently bought a home in the mountains and it is thoroughly infested with rodents, judging by the amount of droppings everywhere. What procedures should we take to clean it up? Is hantavirus a concern?*

From a reader in Colorado

A Yes, hantavirus should be a concern. There are several species of rodents that could inhabit the cabin, including deer mice. You have two options. One is to hire a professional to eradicate the rodents and clean the cabin, which I recommend, and the other is to do it yourself. If you choose the latter, take the following precautions:

- Open up the cabin and let it air out before cleaning.
- Put on a pair of latex rubber gloves, coveralls (disposable, if possible), rubber boots or disposable shoe covers, protective goggles, and an appropriate respiratory protection device, such as a half-mask, air-purifying respirator with a high-efficiency particulate air (HEPA) filter.
- Don't stir up dust by sweeping or vacuuming up droppings or nesting materials. Instead, thoroughly wet contaminated areas with detergent or liquid to deactivate the virus. Most general-purpose disinfectants and household detergents are effective. For large areas, use a 10-percent household laundry bleach solution (about $1^1/2$ cups of bleach per gallon of water).
- Once everything is wet, take up contaminated materials with a damp towel, then mop or sponge the area with disinfectant.
- Spray any dead rodents with disinfectant, then double-bag them along with cleaning materials and bury or burn, or throw out in an appropriate waste disposal system.
- Finally, disinfect gloves before taking them off with disinfectant or soap and water. After taking off the gloves, thoroughly wash hands with soap and warm water. Coveralls should be disposed of or laundered on the site. If no laundry facilities are

available, the coveralls should be immersed in liquid disinfectant until they can be washed.

After the cabin is cleaned, you need to try to seal it to prevent other rodents from entering. You should also initiate a
trapping system to catch any rodents that may still be present. Do not use rodenticides as a rodent may die where it cannot be retrieved. If wood rat nests are present in the cabin,
they should be removed and destroyed. While wood rats are
not known vectors of hantavirus, their nests (middens) are
usually heavily infested with fleas so you may want to treat
accordingly.

Q *One of my customers has packrats. I keep putting out rodenticides,*
which are disappearing, but the packrats seem to be as numerous
as ever. Are they immune to rodenticides and, if so, how do I get
rid of them?

From a reader in Santa Fe, NM

A Packrats aren't immune to rodenticides and they have the disconcerting habit of trading rodenticides for dog food. There
have been cases of packrats taking dog food out of a food bowl
and replacing it with rodenticides left out for them. I never
recommend rodenticides for any rodent control and certainly
not for packrats. Packrats can usually be trapped in Sherman
traps baited with oatmeal and peanut butter. As these are live
traps you will have to dispose of the animal. I would just haul
it off to a more remote location and release it. Word of caution: Don't pet a packrat. They are as cute as buttons but they
can and will bite as would any wild animal.

Q *My exterminator left glueboards in the garage to catch mice. One*
was caught in the trap and suffered for 2 days waiting for the
exterminator to come out and retrieve it. Is there a more humane
way to control mice?

From a reader in San Francisco, CA

A Absolutely! Glueboards should never be used for rodent control for several reasons, the main one being that it causes
unnecessary suffering as you described. I exclusively use

either curiosity traps, which catch mice alive and allow me to release them, or standard snap traps, which kill the mouse quickly and painlessly. I never recommend rodenticides because the mice will almost always die in an inconvenient place resulting in a bad odor. I also would never use glueboards for mouse control because I do not take any pleasure in causing little animals to suffer, even mice. If you have glueboards in your house that were placed by a pest control person to catch mice, throw them away and ask him or her to come out and set standard snap traps. Many pest control companies don't like using snap traps because they appear so simple to use and the customer may think they are not getting their money's worth, or that they can set the traps themselves. By setting out glueboards, which are not readily available to the public, they give the impression they are doing something innovative and instilling the idea of "perceived value" with the customer, which is, of course, utter nonsense.

Snap traps are not always easy to use. Anyone can set a trap but not everyone can catch mice in them. I have seen traps placed backwards, sideways, cattywhumple, and baited with food that a goat wouldn't eat, and these traps have no chance of catching mice. Snap traps should be set perpendicular against a wall with the bait closest to the wall and they should be spaced every 15 feet or so. They should be baited with Tootsie Rolls, gumdrops, or Slim Jims, all favorite foods of mice.

Glueboards, on the other hand, should never be used to catch mice. Even if the person using them is heartless and doesn't care about the suffering of small animals, there is another, very valid reason for not using them. If you live in an area where deer mice are prevalent and hantavirus is a possibility, it could be dangerous to have a mouse stuck in a glueboard for a couple of days defecating and urinating. The hantavirus agent, which is present in feces and urine, can become airborne and spread throughout a room, and thus cause someone in the house to get sick.

When you hire someone to control mice in your house, ask a lot of questions, including how they are going to eradicate the mice. If they say they will use either rodenticides or glueboards, call someone else. A good mouse catcher may be hard to find but it will be worth the effort.

Q *Dear Bugman: I read your column every week and especially appreciate the kind attitude you demonstrate toward insects and living things in general. That tendency of yours—to urge your readers to take a type of wait-and-see attitude before killing every insect that crosses their paths–is especially refreshing.*

I do have a quick question for you, though you don't have to run it in your column. (It may not prove very interesting to others.) My father lives in the Chicago suburbs, and this time of year starts receiving a lot of uninvited mice in the crawl space beneath his home. The crawl space was built under an addition to the house and attaches to his basement. However, the mice never enter the basement, just the crawl space. The outside walls of the crawl space seem impenetrable, and my father has been perplexed for years as to how the mice are getting in. He has taken measures to seal all small openings to the outside to no avail. My father employs a humane trap to capture these rodents so he can release them later. Sometimes, the mouse dies from fear and hopelessness in the trap, and my father is heartbroken. How is it possible for these mice to squeeze through hairline cracks? Any ideas you might have would be much appreciated.

From a reader in Chicago, IL

A I applaud your father for his attitude toward the mice. He must be missing someplace when he sealed the crawl space. A mouse can enter through an opening as small as $1/4$". Have him take another look around and look for the hole they are using. Until he finds and seals that last hole or two, the problem will persist. Good luck!

Q *I have gerbils loose in my house. How can I catch them and return them to their cages without harming them?*

A You can make your own gerbil trap (which will work for mice, both wild and domesticated). Take a big stainless steel bowl and smear the inside of it with butter or grease. Place some bait in the bottom of the bowl. Tootsie rolls, oatmeal, peanut butter, or all three together will work. Then place a couple of wooden ramps along the outside of the bowl. The gerbils (or mice) will crawl up the ramps and jump into the bowl to get the bait but will be unable to get out because of the slippery sides.

A similar trap can be made for cockroaches, but instead of wooden ramps you would use broom straws placed close together and instead of food as a bait, you would use beer. The roaches will climb the straws to get at the beer and will fall in when reaching the end of the straws that will be over the bowl.

Prairie Dogs

Q *One of my customers has about a half dozen prairie dogs on his property and wants me to gas them. Is there another method of controlling prairie dogs or do they need control?*

A I contacted one of the leading experts on prairie dogs in the Southwest, Ana Davidson from the University of New Mexico, and asked her to respond to this question as I consider it very important. Here is her reply:

> Prairie dogs are large, colonial, ground-nesting squirrels, and their colonies are important habitats for many other animals. Prior to the early 1900s, prairie dogs were among the most numerous and widespread animals in native North American grassland ecosystems. However, mass extermination programs, introduced bubonic plague, unregulated sport shooting, and extensive habitat loss have reduced prairie dogs to less than 1 percent of their former numbers. Human-caused declines in prairie dog populations have threatened or endangered other animals that are dependent upon prairie dogs, including the black-footed ferret, burrowing owl, and ferruginous hawk.
>
> Despite their importance, people often want to exterminate prairie dogs because of misconcep-

tions about proliferation, children being bitten, destruction of landscaped areas, or plague. Prairie dogs are not prolific breeders. They only have one litter per year, consisting of about four young, of which only two usually survive. Prairie dogs are not a threat to children. They are timid animals, and when approached by humans, prairie dogs quickly scurry into the safety of their burrows.

Prairie dogs do not carry the plague; fleas carry the plague. These fleas can be found on many wild animals, and are not limited to prairie dogs. Killing prairie dogs just causes fleas to search for another host, and is not recommended by the Centers for Disease Control and Prevention (CDC) as an effective method of plague control. The key to preventing plague is to control fleas, not prairie dogs. Plague can be successfully prevented by avoiding contact with dead animals and dusting pets and rodent burrows with flea powder (personal communication, CDC). Plague is also easily overcome with antibiotics when detected early, so people should educate themselves about the symptoms of plague. A colony of active prairie dogs is actually indicative of healthy, plague-free prairie dogs, and should not cause concern *(http://www.cdc.gov/ncidod /dvbid/plagen.htm)*.

If prairie dogs are causing damage to landscaped areas, you can use visual barriers and additional below-ground barriers to contain the animals. Prairie dogs are highly discouraged by tall vegetation, so plant native shrubs and do not mow native grasses. Xeriscaping the area will also help discourage prairie dogs, and conserve water.

Rat poison should not be used to kill prairie dogs because it causes secondary poisoning of dogs, cats, and other animals. The only legal method for killing prairie dogs involves the use of poisonous gas by licensed professionals (in most states), which is costly. The poisonous gases used are inhumane, causing slow and painful deaths, and can take up to 72 hours to induce death in an animal. In the meantime, symptoms range from burning of the mucus membranes to paralysis. The best recommendation is to learn to live with these native animals and, if for some reason, prairie dogs must be removed, I recommend contacting a local wildlife organization that relocates prairie dogs.

For more information, see the following websites: *http:// prairiedogs.org/ and http://prairiedogpals.bigstep.com/homepage .htm.*

Snakes

Q *Help! This might be out of your area, but I need help before my wife sees this. It'd take me a month to get everything out of my garage.*
  The snake is about 2' to 2.5' long, pink or light orange, and moves like a sidewinder (I think). What is it? Is it dangerous? How do I trap, kill, or get it to leave? Many thanks for any help.
  From a reader in Albuquerque, NM

A What you have described sounds like a young coachwhip (or red racer). These snakes are completely harmless although they get a little testy if you pick them up. It will probably nail a few mice in your garage and leave on its own. I doubt if your wife will ever see it, but you could explain to her that the only dangerous snakes in New Mexico have rattles. For the purists, we do have a little coral snake in the extreme southwest portion of the state, but it is very small, inoffensive, and uncommon, and I have never heard of it biting anyone, so I do not consider it a "dangerous" snake (although it is venomous).

Q *I live in Virginia in a rural area. I have three children under the age of seven. My yard has been plagued by copperhead snakes. We killed two in May 2000. Also killed two last summer. Since it is only June, I feel that we are bound to see more during the upcoming summer months.*

Can you give me any suggestions as to what we can do that would make our yard safe for the children? We do not live in a mountainous area but do have woods on two sides. Please help. Thank you.

From a reader in Virginia

A There is a product available that may be helpful to you. It is called Snake-Away and it is a mothball-like product that snakes do not crawl over. It is more effective against slow crawling snakes such as copperheads than fast-moving snakes such as whipsnakes and racers.

Make sure that there aren't flat boards, rocks, or similar objects on the ground in your yard that may offer harborage for snakes.

Copperheads have fairly weak venom and I don't know of any fatalities that can be attributed to their bite. I was bitten a number of years ago by a copperhead (it was my fault, not the snake's), and I was hospitalized for four days and have a crooked finger to show for it.

If you purchase Snake-Away, place it along your yard boundaries that border on the woods. Four pounds of Snake-Away will treat about 250 linear feet, so that will help you determine how much you need.

Squirrels

Q *Dear bug person, I know that your expertise lies in insects but I am desperate. I live on the bluff above the river and I have squirrels by the dozens. They are very destructive, eating all my plants, especially tomatoes when they first start to ripen. I don't really want to kill them but for two years, I used the Havahart trap and they died in there immediately, probably from the stress. Do you have any ideas about discouraging them from coming into my space? Their holes are all over the bluff and it seems that it would be weakened by the tunneling. Of course, they carry fleas and the thought of bubonic plague is not a happy one. I would appreciate any help you can give me. I enjoy your column. Thank you.*

From a reader in Cedar Crest, NM

A You seem to have no trouble trapping the squirrels, which is good. You can do one of two things. Either switch to Sherman traps, which are enclosed and dark, or place a towel over the Havahart (except for the entrance). The squirrels get stressed because they are trapped and aware they are helpless to outside influences. In a Sherman trap or covered Havahart they will not be able to see out of the trap and will thus develop a false sense of security; they will be fine in the trap as long as there is food. You can then release them in an area where they won't bother anyone. Caution: Do not handle them unless absolutely necessary and wear gloves and a long-sleeved shirt to avoid flea bites. Ground squirrels may have fleas that can be vectors for the plague.

Voles

Q *I had emailed you several weeks ago about the tunnels in my garden and the destruction of my plants. In speaking with my neighbors, these critters have been identified as voles. Now we need your help as how to get rid of them. Maybe some poison in the small holes they make in the soil? All help will be greatly appreciated. Looking forward to hearing from you.*

From a reader in Boulder, CO

A To thrive and increase their numbers, voles require cover and ready access to food. Mowing lawns and weedy areas, and periodically spading or tilling a garden reduces the available cover favored by voles. Mulches, which also provide cover, should be cleared away at least 3' from the base of susceptible trees and shrubs to impede bark feeding. If vole injury is serious to overwintered perennials, such as strawberries, mulching should be delayed until after the ground has frozen.

Individual plants can be protected from vole injury by tree guards or wire mesh screening, 1/4" or less in diameter. Because voles can tunnel, the barriers should be buried at least 6". Placing small, sharp pebbles in planting holes for bulbs also deters voles. During the winter, compacting the snow around plants serves as a barrier to vole tunneling.

Mousetraps, placed with the trigger along the runway, can be used to kill voles. Baiting the traps is not necessary if the traps are properly placed in the runways.

Hot-pepper mixtures and thiram-based repellents have been registered for control of voles, although their effectiveness is considered questionable.

6

Pest Control Services and Pesticides

🦗 This chapter is devoted to questions about pesticides and the pest control industry. Many of the questions and answers may be controversial but only to pest control companies who are less than competent or less than ethical. The vast majority of people in the pest control industry are hard-working and honest practitioners of their trade. In the last two questions in this chapter, I ask Johnna to provide her opinions on pesticides.

Q *I called several exterminators to get bids on controlling waterbugs. One wanted to come every month, another four times a year, and one said he would come only when I wanted him. Is there one plan that is more effective than the others?*

From a reader in Albuquerque, NM

A The frequency of the service is not important, as frequency is based solely on the economic needs of the exterminator. Most companies use monthly service to generate monthly income, but you will probably spend about the same amount of money over a year no matter which service you choose. Pick your service based on substance. It is better to have someone come out every month and only use pesticides if absolutely necessary than have someone come out four times a year or less and hose down your house inside and out. I would never recommend anyone who simply sprays your baseboards every month. Always check references with the companies bidding for your business.

Q *The cable guy needs to go under my house to do some work. He wants me to get the crawl space sprayed to kill all the bugs. What do you recommend?*

From a reader in Albuquerque, NM

A I recommend you get a cable guy who isn't afraid of a few bugs. There is no good way to rid a crawl space of insects and spiders. If you use an insecticidal dust, you will kill a few of the crawling insects but will not get the ones under debris or in cracks and no one wants to crawl through a layer of insecticidal dusts or even noninsecticidal dusts. Liquid pesticides would be useless as well and the fumes from them would filter into the house. Even the so-called odorless pesticides give off fumes. The only difference is that you don't realize they are there and don't know how they are affecting you. Foggers are not a good method of controlling bugs in a crawl space either. The foggers may kill any bugs within a couple of feet of them but beyond that most creepy crawlies will escape the chemical. I would suggest you take a broom and knock down any spiders and their webs from around the crawl space entrance and any you can reach immediately inside the entrance, where most of the spider activity will be taking place. Then you can tell the cable guy you would rather have a few bugs under your house than a lot of potentially dangerous pesticides.

Q *I manage a day care center. We have occasional large roaches, spiders, ants, and mice. How can we control these pests without endangering the children with pesticides?*

From a reader in Albuquerque, NM

A Whenever you do pest control where children are present you have to be extremely careful. You should try not to use any pesticides if possible, but if you have to, they should be used on weekends when no children are present. If you use baits on weekends it is imperative that you come in early Monday and pick up all the excess bait products and any dead insects before any children get there. Do not leave any pesticides around even if you think they are in a child-proof area. The only exception would be the kitchen, assuming it is locked when the kitchen staff isn't around.

The building must be properly sealed to prevent incidental pest entry. Doors and windows should close tightly and screens should be in good repair. Doors without screens should never be left open. The large cockroaches can only enter the facility from the outside or from the drains. If the building is sealed, they won't be able to get in from the outside. You have to make sure the drain covers are in place at night to prevent them from coming up the drains. If you have floor drains that don't have covers, then fill a zip-lock bag with water and place it on the drain.

If you are having ants, then you should spray them with soap and water every time you see them. They will disappear in a week or so because you are continually depleting the colony. Check around the perimeter of the facility and the playground for ants. You can pour boiling water down the anthills to discourage them. Do not use granular ant bait outside as the children may pick it up and put it in their mouths.

All of the ends of the hollow pipes used in the construction of swing sets, monkey bars, etc. should be sealed or screened to prevent wasps from nesting in the pipes. Used tires on the playground should be hosed out every morning as this is a good hiding place for spiders and other crawling insects. If you find mice in the building you should only use live traps to catch them. Rodenticides are absolutely out of the question in a day care facility and snap traps and glueboards are rather unpleasant to use around children.

One of the best tools you can use is a vacuum cleaner. You can vacuum up any spider or occasional insect that wanders in as well as any dead insects. Before you use the vacuum on live bugs, suck up some diatomaceous earth first as this will kill the insects in the bag.

If you have to use pesticides or if you hire a pest control company to use pesticides, you should notify all parents beforehand in case their children are sensitive to chemicals. They may want to make other arrangements for their children for a few days. Make sure you have labels and Material Safety Data Sheets available for any pesticides you use.

Every day care center (and school) should have a pest

management policy statement in place at all times. Only integrated pest management procedures similar to those outlined above should be used. Never, ever spray chemicals along baseboards in the facility where children are present (or anywhere else for that matter) and never allow chemicals to be sprayed around the perimeter of the building for "preventive" measures. Sealing the building properly will help keep the bugs out.

Q *I am thinking about changing exterminators after the holidays. There are dozens of ads in the phone book. Do you have any suggestions for narrowing them down? What should I look for in a phone book ad?*

From a reader in Chicago, IL

A There are several things to be aware of. If someone advertises they use "safe insecticides" or "safe chemicals" you should be cautious. They are oxymorons. There is no such thing as a safe insecticide or chemical. They can be applied safely, but they are not "safe." If someone advertises "odorless chemicals," you should also be cautious. It doesn't mean a chemical is safe because you can't smell it. Nerve gas is odorless. Watch out for what I would call over-enthusiastic claims. For instance, if someone advertises they can control "all insects" or "all crawling insects," I would consider that a bit of a stretch. You would have to use a lot of insecticides to fulfill those claims, notwithstanding the fact that most insects, including crawling insects, are beneficial and need no control.

After separating the wheat from the chaff in the advertisements, you should call three or four companies and let them come to your house and give you a bid. Don't hesitate to ask lots of questions as they should know the answers. Be cautious of anyone who wants to give you a price over the phone. You wouldn't expect a mechanic, a plumber, or a doctor to give you a quote for their services over the phone, so why would you expect someone who is potentially going to use insecticides in your home to do so? Every home is different and most do not need insecticidal treatments. This can only be determined by a careful and thorough inspection from a qualified and ethical pest management professional.

Q *You always seem to offer alternatives to pesticides in your column. Are pesticides ever necessary?*

From a reader in San Francisco, CA

A Of course they are. I promote the practice of IPM (integrated pest management), which uses a variety of methods to control a pest, including the judicious use of pesticides when other means are exhausted. I also promote the use of baits, particularly against roaches and ants, and baits are insecticides. Baits, however, are designed to eliminate specific pests and not kill a broad range of insects as do liquid insecticides, and baits can easily be placed in areas where nontarget organisms (kids and pets) can't reach them.

I do not support the spray-and-pray method of pest control where someone indiscriminately sprays chemicals on baseboards and around the foundation of a home and all of the soil adjacent to the foundation and calls that pest control. In my opinion, this is pesticide pollution. This method subscribes to the theory that large amounts of pesticides will kill lots of bugs. Basically, they spray chemicals and pray it works; no science here.

Q *You always say we should never have our homes sprayed around the outside. If it keeps pests away, why not? What harm does it do?*

From a reader in Rio Rancho, NM

A I don't believe spraying pesticides on the soil around a home or business is a good idea for several reasons. First, 99 percent of the pesticides sprayed around the foundation never come in contact with a pest and the chemicals may actually do more harm than good. Most of the pesticides seep into the ground where they will kill organisms such as oribatid mites, springtails, and other microfauna that are necessary to the health of the soil. The chemical that remains on the surface breaks down fairly quickly because of climatic conditions, making it ineffective against pests, while the pesticides that have leached into the ground continue to kill all sorts of good bugs over an extended period of time.

We have a history of destroying what we need and we should start to use alternative means to achieve some of our goals. Habitat modification is a much better method of keeping pests away from our homes than spraying chemicals all over the place. It should not be necessary to destroy thousands of beneficial soil organisms (which carry out the decomposition of organic material and the transformation of organic nutrients into mineral forms usable by plants) in order to kill the odd centipede or cricket.

If you have to have the outside of your house chemically treated, insist that the pest control operator only apply pesticides to cracks and crevices where pests may hide. Places such as expansion joints or cracks in the sidewalk or around door jambs are good areas to treat. Do not let them spray the soil around your house.

Q *I noticed your article in last Wednesday's* San Francisco Chronicle *(9/13/00). Your website doesn't seem to have my answer so I am writing to you directly.*

The problem: I am 47, HIV+ for a long time, and my immune system is compromised (currently around 151 t-cells). I now get major allergic reactions to bites (mosquitoes, fleas, etc.). Over the last six months I've been getting more and more bites.

I put up screens, never see a mosquito, or feel its bite—so we (my doctor and I) don't think it's mosquitoes. The cat sleeps on the bed, but I put Advantage on her regularly and she doesn't scratch like a cat with fleas. (In another location, there were fleas in a bed from cats and I felt them move on me, and that's not happening here.)

The only thing left I can think of is spider bites (BTW, I never feel myself being bitten). The garden has tons of spiders and first thing in the morning I'm always running into a web strung from a tree to a plant or between patio chairs. The garage is full of them. It takes no time for a small area cleaned of cobwebs (windows or boxes in storage), to be covered with cobwebs again (I've only seen daddy longlegs). In the living area of the house I see them periodically (different types, small, medium), and infrequently walk through a web string in the house that I can't see. Are they out at night crawling around, on my bed, and mistaking me for a nice meal?

Solutions: Ask anyone how to get rid of spiders in the garden or house and they say, "Don't do it. Spiders are so beneficial and eat many other pests." No one seems to know how to kill spiders—

and I'm beginning to think that's why they say "live with them"! There doesn't appear to be any nonprofessional spray to kill spiders. Do I need to have the house fumigated (I rent)?

Can you offer any suggestions? Is it really the spiders (does it sound like it's spiders to you?) or could it be something else we haven't considered? With my immune system wrecked, I have a big overblown response to these bug bites, and one or two a month is really getting frustrating!

From a reader in San Francisco, CA

A I don't think spiders are biting you. Although spiders may bite if they are handled, they rarely bite for no reason at all and usually you can feel the bite. It may be small, biting flies known as no-see-ums.

I suggest you get a pest management professional to completely inspect your home, even if it means setting up light traps and see what is living there. If the professional does not find anything, then I suggest you visit a dermatologist who can do tests to determine if the bites contain saliva or venom of some sort. Another possibility is that you may have delusory parasitosis, a condition in which people get "bites" they can't identify or their doctor can't identify and blame them on unknown bugs. Many other things can produce "bites" in people, such as fibers from new carpets and slivers of paper from a copier. A whole assortment of household chemicals could be forming bite-like sores if you are allergic to the ingredients.

What you don't need to do is to fumigate your house. Keep me posted; I want to use this in my column, as your dilemma is a very serious issue.

Q *You have mentioned* Bacillus thuringiensis *a number of times in your column. What exactly is it, how does it work, and what does it control?*

From a reader in Detroit, MI

A *Bacillus thuringiensis* (Bt) is a commercially available bacteria that causes disease in certain insects. It was discovered in 1911 in Thuringia, Germany, infecting Mediterranean flour moths. At least 35 varieties of Bt have subsequently been identified, each affecting different groups of insects. Manufacturers have marketed a number of strains of Bt as it has been extremely successful in controlling a large number of pests.

Bt is a stomach poison that must be eaten by the target insect to be toxic. Bt works by disrupting the gut lining of susceptible insects, eventually killing them by starvation or blood poisoning. Infected insects shrivel and darken before they die. Bt is very safe for humans, pets, and nontarget organisms as it is very host specific. There are a number of brands available on the market for a variety of insects.

Because Bt is a living organism, it must be protected from high temperatures. Ideally Bt should be stored in a refrigerator or cooler. Bt powders will remain active for two or three years if stored properly. The powders are mixed with water and applied as sprays. Do not make up more than you can use at one time as a Bt solution loses its effectiveness in 12 to 72 hours, depending on which formulation you use.

Q *You mention diatomaceous earth occasionally. What exactly is it and how does it work?*

From a reader in Oklahoma City, OK

A Diatomaceous earth (DE) is mined from the fossilized silica shell remains of unicellular or colonial algae, known as diatoms. It has both abrasive and sorptive qualities. DE absorbs the waxy layer on the surface of the insect's skins, causing the insect to desiccate or dry out. It addition, it works as an abrasive and ruptures insect cuticles, allowing cell sap to leak out.

DE is formulated as a dust and is virtually nontoxic to mammals. Both swimming pool-grade DE, which is used as a filtering agent, and natural DE come from the same sources, but are processed differently. Swimming pool-grade DE contains crystalline silica, which can be a respiratory hazard. Always use natural DE if possible when controlling insects.

Diatomaceous earth is very effective against a large number of pests, including roaches, ants, bedbugs, stored-product pests, fleas, ticks, spiders, wasps, snails, slugs, and many others.

It should be available in hardware stores or home-builders centers. If you can't find any in the area, contact me and I will give you the names of several suppliers.

Q *Are the bug bombs sold in stores safe to use?*

From a reader in Tucson, AZ

A I never recommend those things but if you have to use them read the directions very carefully. Recently a lady in Arizona set off a couple of those aerosol bombs in her home and neglected to turn off the pilot lights as the directions on the can stated. The bug bombs acted like real bombs as one door was blown off its frame. Even if you use a can of spray to kill a cockroach you have to be careful. In another incident a woman used a whole can of bug spray to kill one roach. She neglected to clean up the residue on the floor and later slipped, breaking her hip. If you have to use store-bought pesticides (and I can think of no reason why you would have to), then please read all of the directions very carefully.

NOTE: The following two questions are from me to Johnna Lachnit to get her opinion on pesticides and pesticide use.

Q *I know you are against the indiscriminate use of pesticides, as I am. What are some of the reasons for this, and do you believe pesticides have a place in our society?*

A Pesticide use is a very complex subject for me. My personal opinion is that pesticide use is unnecessary and has no place in society. I also feel that many people are so self-centered and egotistical that they honestly believe humans have dominion over this Earth and that the Earth and the other planets shall be conquered. The question is then: How can we conquer what gives us life and in essence is a part of our very being? We have lost touch with our connection to the animals, the Earth, and the elements. We have forgotten that when you break everything down to the smallest particle that we are all truly the same. Fears and selfish desires control how we look at everything. Many people are obsessed with making things clean and sterile and the chemical industry willingly provides lots of means to reach that end.

Everyone has free agency to make their own choices; while I wish people didn't feel a need to use pesticides I know most do. But it remains important to point out that pesticide use in most cases is absolutely unnecessary. We prove this all the time, even by showing that there are techniques to have a high crop output of organically grown foods. I don't deny that there are some instances where pesticides can be the last resort and very helpful. But such use is rare and far removed from pesticides applied because people feel the need to kill creatures out of their own fears.

We have truly lost touch with life. Our comfort has become isolation from the Earth, and if parts of the Earth such as insects invade our lives, we must destroy them. We see life outside ourselves as a potential plague. It isn't, and I hope the use of pesticides declines. The use of pesticides not only hurts our environment but us as well. We forget the delicate balance of life and how all life exists within itself with no one thing above the other. We are our own enemies, not the little insects that crawl within the soil. Thus, we should only use pesticides if absolutely necessary, that is, when there is no other alternative available. Still, I believe that the general alternative to pesticides is to have a little more faith in the planet we have been blessed with rather than in the products of corporations that play on our fears.

Like everyone else, I am not perfect, but I strive to be of better service to this planet and all life, not just my own. For my life is dependent on all life around me, and the death of my body is not the death of my soul. However, the death of my soul shall come if I can't love and respect all life. If we could see ourselves as a single entity because all life is of the same essence, then we could see that our chronic self-mutilation shall lead to our own suicide. Everything alive is part of a cycle of creation, and we must learn to accept our species' part in that cycle.

Johnna Lachnit

Q *What do you consider the misuse of a pesticide? Can you give readers an example?*

A My answer to the previous question reveals how I feel about using pesticides. But, I'll address this brief answer to those who insist on using them. Two things aggravate me. One is when we use pesticides when an alternative is available. The other is baseboard spraying and frequent spraying of chemicals that we are well aware have residual effects on ourselves and other creatures. How many parents are aware of the days and times their children's school buildings and grounds are sprayed? Is your child a toddler who likes to touch and taste everything? How much of the chemicals ends up in the food in the cafeterias? I would be more concerned about these issues than the cockroach crawling across the floor. Cockroaches are harmless and are actually very clean. Parents need to pay attention to what can really harm their children—indiscriminate use of pesticides.

Johnna Lachnit

7

Delusory Parasitosis

🐞 Of all the bug calls I get, the most frustrating are from people who suffer from delusory parasitosis (DP). I try to explain to them what DP is: a condition in which the patient believes that insects or mites are crawling on, biting, or burrowing in the skin, when no arthropod is present. Typically, by the time they get to me they have already been to several doctors who tell them they have a rash caused by an unknown agent. Occasionally a physician will examine a patient and tell him or her that an insect or mite caused the lesions, and then recommend that a pest control operator treat his or her home. Conscientious pest control operators will make an inspection and then refuse to treat if no target pest is found. Less ethical pest control companies will treat homes regardless of whether a target pest is found, which only exacerbates the problem as the pesticides may have a negative effect on an already sensitive person.

In reality, there are two separate conditions: DP (i.e., delusions of parasitosis) and illusory parasitosis (i.e., illusions of parasitosis). In the first, the patient believes that there are living organisms in or on the skin. In illusory parasitosis, skin lesions may be occurring but they are from stimuli other than arthropods, although the patient is convinced they are caused by bugs. Clinically, it is important for medical personnel to separate these conditions in order to properly treat them. In this book, I lump them together under the term "delusory parasitosis," which is more commonly used.

Below are some examples of correspondence I have received from people suffering from delusory parasitosis.

Q *I feel little things crawling on me constantly. An exterminator suggested I may have dust mites and he could control them by spraying and fogging my home. Would this treatment work for these mites?*

From a reader in Albuquerque, NM

A I suggest you go to a dermatologist and find out what is causing you to feel "little things" crawling on you. Dust mites are not common in the Southwest and the exterminator should lose his license for even suggesting such a treatment.

House dust mites live on bacteria associated with skin flakes and are fairly common in the eastern United States. They depend on high humidity, above about 60 percent, to obtain needed moisture. When they are found in this area it is usually in bedrooms where humidifiers are continuously running. Reducing humidity is the most effective way to eliminate populations of dust mites. Vacuuming areas around bedding or other areas where skin flakes are commonly shed is also effective. If humidifiers have to be used, then the mattress and pillows should be encased in plastic to prevent the mites. Pesticides have not been proven to have any value in controlling dust mites and I would urge you not to let the exterminator spray and fog your home. The pesticides may do far more damage to you than any mites, real or imagined.

Q *I saw your reply to my question in* [Albuquerque] Tribune, *dated October 5. Thank you. After I wrote to you, I talked to more pest control men. One told me immediately that I had a "parasite that was feeding on my body" and to see a doctor.*

With this information, I visited two doctors, pharmacists, etc.—they had never heard of this. I was very depressed. . . . Finally, I had some leftover antibiotics from an illness, so I took some for three or four days. I think "they" are gone, and I am feeling much better.

My daughter searched on the Internet and gave me the papers I am sending you. If I have more symptoms, I will try a dermatologist. I find it alarming that in this large city, the doctors could not help me. Thank you for your time.

From a reader in Albuquerque, NM

A I am glad you will see a dermatologist, as I suggested originally, if the symptoms return. The fact sheet you sent from the Internet is from a group called "National Unidentified Skin Parasite Association (NUSPA)," and contains "information" on "Unidentified Skin Parasitic Infection (USPI)."

I consulted with a number of entomologists and medical doctors about this problem and the consensus is that this condition is known as delusory, delusional, or psychogenic parasitosis and is a well-described mental health problem. Typically, patients affected are elderly women with failing eyesight. It is not unusual for relatively young women to have this, but it is rare in males. The usual symptoms are "bites" and "itching" that are attributed to very small "parasites" or "mites" perceived as "tiny specks" that can "jump away before they can be caught." The patients' stories can be quite compelling, and their pleas for help and assistance are genuine.

Patients typically approach pest control operators (PCOs) first and request that they spray their homes. Of course, it's both illegal (in most states) and unethical to treat for a presumptive problem with no verified pest being present. In most cases, when the PCO route proves to be ineffective, the person suffering from delusory parasitosis (DP) may start to self-treat their premises with insecticides and some have made themselves quite ill by overtreatment. At about the same time, they try to get in touch with an entomologist and bring them samples of their "bugs," which almost always turn out to be pieces of skin scabs, debris, and bits of fabric. Family members often develop the condition and become facilitators, stating that they have the parasites also. People suffering from DP vigorously resist any notion that the problem is mental and insist they are suffering from some sort of insect attack. They insist they are not "imagining" this.

From an entomological standpoint, the best course is to route these folks to dermatology/internal medicine as quickly as possible. There are certain metabolic disorders that can make people feel like things are biting them or crawling on their skin, and when these are resolved their "parasites" vanish. For those with more severe psychological problems, there are some new psychotropic drugs that help, but need to be monitored by physicians with the proper background.

The Web page you sent appears to have been constructed by someone affected by the syndrome or in a facilitator role. It has all the markings of the "they-won't-believe-me" approach so common in these cases. When they find skin lesions difficult to identify, dermatologists and medical parasitologists often do "punch" skin biopsies that they send to a pathologist. This way, it is impossible for an "unknown" parasitic invertebrate to be overlooked as the Web page alleges.

🐞 **Below are two more letters from people suffering from DP. I reprint them to illustrate the desperation these people are experiencing.**

Q *I don't have a bug to send as we can't see them. They are making my life miserable.*

They seem to appear at night, especially after we turn on the lights. They invade my hair, eyes, nose, and mouth. I think they are very tiny white bugs, and they must fly.

We have tried everything—citronella candles, fly strips, sprays, etc. We have called insect control companies—one man said they were called "no-see-me" bugs. There must be another name! Hope you can help. Thanks.

From a reader in Michigan

Q *Something is biting me, and it's very itchy. I can't see these bugs but I know they're there because they bite me. I washed my bedding and vacuumed everything but they are still there. I live next to an old corn field where they are building. Could this be the problem?*

P.S. I don't have any vegetation around my house.

From a reader in Illinois

🐞 **This next letter is particularly sad. According to the postmark, it came from Albuquerque, New Mexico. It was scribbled on a torn piece of legal pad paper and was unsigned.**

Q *Occasionally, I work in a garden center area. The chemicals from bug killers, fertilizers, and weed killers are killing me! I get a headache, nausea, and burning in my chest and throat!*

They think I am finicky and making it up. The next day my windpipe area "peels." No one else minds. They say, "I've gotten used to the smell," "Doesn't bother me," and these people work there all the time!! I work there once or twice a week! It's not the smell that worries me! It's the long-term damage that it's doing to my lungs!!!

There is also exposure to magnetic fields all the time. I feel this can cause cancer. No one cares! No one at work listens—the company won't either.

Hope you print a (loud) article on these dangers.

P.S.: Regarding foggers, I did not know we were supposed to extinguish pilot lights until I was reading the instructions. I then chose not to purchase it. People need to be more alerted to these things like on TV. Not everyone reads the paper except me.

8

Multiple Chemical Sensitivity

Ann McCampbell is a medical doctor who used to work in the field of women's health. Prior to becoming disabled with multiple chemical sensitivity (MCS) in 1989, she was also a musician and competitive beach volleyball player. Now she is chronically ill; she can only eat a handful of foods, and rarely leaves her home in order to avoid exposures to perfume, pesticides, new carpets, smoke, cleaning products, and other chemicals. Like many people with MCS, she has struggled to obtain safe housing and at times had to live in her car, a makeshift tent, and on a mat in her backyard. When exposed to problematic chemicals, she typically experiences headache, nausea, abdominal pain, fatigue, and an irregular heartbeat.

For the past five years, Dr. McCampbell has been chair of the MCS Task Force of New Mexico. This is a statewide, grassroots advocacy organization comprised of and for chemically sensitive New Mexicans. It is dedicated to advocating for chemically sensitive people, increasing awareness of MCS, and educating others about the hazards of high- and low-level chemical exposures, especially the hazards of pesticides. The MCS Task Force supports mandatory school integrated pest management (IPM), notification requirements for all pesticide use, and a reporting system to keep track of pesticide use in the state. School IPM would reduce children's exposures to pesticides, and general notification would allow people to make informed choices about whether to expose themselves to pesticides. The Task Force believes that the less people are exposed to pesticides, the less chance they will develop MCS and other health problems, and the greater the chance they will remain healthy and productive.

People with multiple chemical sensitivities (MCS) are made sick by exposures to low levels of many common chemicals. Substances that frequently cause symptoms in those with MCS are pesticides, perfume, tobacco smoke, fresh paint, binding and glue in or under new carpets, air "fresheners," chemicals used in many building materials, vehicle exhaust, solvents, industrial fumes, and many cleaning compounds. Reactions can occur if these substances are inhaled, ingested, or absorbed through the skin. Symptoms range from mild to life-threatening and include, but are not limited to, headache, trouble concentrating, nausea, vomiting, diarrhea, fatigue, weakness, dizziness, numbness and tingling, wheezing, irregular heartbeat, tremors, seizures, and joint and muscle pain. MCS symptoms in children include red cheeks and ears, dark circles under the eyes, hyperactivity, and behavior or learning problems. People with MCS also often react to foods, drugs, molds, and pollen, and some react to electromagnetic fields.

Many people who develop MCS were once healthy individuals who tolerated chemical exposures like everyone else, until they had an exposure from which they did not recover. For example, people have developed MCS after moving into a newly built house, having carpet installed or other remodeling work done in their office, or after having their home sprayed with pesticides. Others slowly become ill over a period of years, seemingly as a result of the cumulative exposures of everyday life. Exposures to organophosphate pesticides are the most implicated in causing MCS. Pesticide exposures have increasingly been linked to other health problems as well, such as prostate and breast cancer, leukemia, Parkinson's and Alzheimer's disease, asthma, and decreasing sperm counts.

Increasing numbers of people are becoming chemically sensitive. Random population-based surveys conducted by the departments of health in California and New Mexico found that 16 percent of respondents reported being unusually sensitive to common chemicals, such as pesticides. Women were twice as likely as men to report being chemically sensitive. Otherwise, chemically sensitive respondents were evenly distributed among age groups, education and income levels, and areas of the state. The percentage of those reporting chemical sensitivity were similar among ethnic and racial groups, except for Native Americans, who reported a higher prevalence (27 percent in New Mexico). Two and 3.5 percent of respondents in New Mexico and California, respectively, reported having been diagnosed with MCS, the most severe form of chemical sensitivity.

MCS is thought to result from a neurotoxic injury that damages a person's brain and/or nervous system. SPECT and PET brain scans, electroencephalograms (EEG), and neuropsychological tests often demonstrate abnormal brain function in people with MCS. The immune and hormonal systems are also often affected. While everyone is at risk of becoming chemically sensitive, those who regularly work with neurotoxic chemicals, such as pesticides, solvents, and formaldehyde-emitting building materials, are thought to be at increased risk.

People with MCS react to a wide variety of pesticides, including insecticides (organophosphates, pyrethroids, and carbamates), herbicides, fungicides, and fumigants. Pesticides are toxic to everyone to some degree, but chemically sensitive people react adversely to much lower levels of pesticides than healthy people. Exposures to even minute amounts of pesticides can cause severe symptoms and prolonged relapses in the most chemically sensitive people. For example, a chemically sensitive woman driving along a street sprayed with herbicides weeks earlier became so nauseated, weak, and confused that she could not find her way home. Another woman was hospitalized for vomiting blood after an herbicide was sprayed in her neighbor's yard. A chemically sensitive boy vomited when he tried to play Little League baseball on a field that was treated with herbicides. A woman developed nausea, dizziness, numbness, tingling, and an irregular heartbeat after eating conventionally grown food, which contains traces of pesticides, rather than organically grown food. And a chemically sensitive man developed tremors, memory problems, and prolonged fatigue after moving into a house that was sprayed with pesticides years earlier.

There is a range of severity of chemical sensitivities from those only mildly affected to those severely affected with full-blown MCS. MCS is recognized as a potentially disabling condition by the Social Security Administration and the U.S. Department of Housing and Urban Development (HUD). It is also covered under the Americans with Disabilities Act (ADA) on a case-by-case basis. That means that employers, schools, hospitals, and other public places are required to provide reasonable accommodations to chemically sensitive people when the presence of pesticides or new carpets, paint, fragrances, or other chemicals create an access barrier. These substances commonly present a barrier for chemically sensitive people, which prevents them from going into many offices, stores, schools, hospitals, hotels, buses, banks, theaters, places of worship, and other buildings. Substituting nonvolatile baits and pest-exclusion methods for routine pesticide spraying in these buildings helps to increase access for the chemically sensitive and to protect the health of all occupants.

The growing numbers of people becoming chemically sensitive are helping to encourage pest control operators (PCOs) to switch from routine pesticide praying to less-toxic IPM. Some in the business, however, are resistant to change, and like pesticide manufacturers, "would rather fight than switch." In other words, they would rather deny that people with MCS react to low levels of chemicals than question the safety of pesticides. But members of the pest control industry would be better served to heed the message that pesticides are not safe, since more than one pest control applicator has developed MCS from work-related exposure.

Some PCOs feel so threatened by MCS that they have lobbied against MCS-related legislation, whether or not it is related to pest control. This is unfortunate, since people with MCS urgently need help in obtaining accessible housing, employment, and health care. PCO opposition to MCS is also misguided since people with MCS are supportive of the pest control industry, though not of widespread pesticide use. The goal of reducing the use of toxic pesticides does not, in fact, threaten the pest control industry. To the contrary, IPM programs that do not rely on these pesticides and are recommended by the MCS community require more assistance from knowledgeable pest control professionals, not less. People with MCS want to see pest control professionals paid well for their expertise and not just for applying pesticides. The MCS community also supports the pest control industry's position that there should be more restrictions on the general public's pesticide use. And last but not least, when PCOs use less toxic pesticides as recommended by people with MCS, their actions help protect their own health and the health of their families.

Q *I am a homeowner and have regular pest control spraying in and around the house. I also have a weakened immune system and want to find alternative ways of controlling pests.*

I use ****** Pest Control. The usual application here is 1 gallon of .015-percent Demand CS; Niban granules inside the house; and outside, Max Force granules. I have crickets (harmless, I like them), black widow spiders, scorpions, springtail fleas in the bathtub drains, and other typical insects. The house is two to two-and-a-half years old.

From a reader in Rio Rancho, NM

A If you have a weakened immune system, you don't need any of those pesticides around, especially the liquid product. Niban granules in the house will kill the crickets (which you like), cockroaches, and silverfish, and is probably the safest material this person used. The springtails (not fleas) can easily be killed with soap and water. You can keep the spiders and scorpions out by making sure your doors and windows close tightly. If either enters your home occasionally as they will, you can simply kill them individually by smashing them or vacuuming them up.

Q *A store that I frequent regularly uses a pesticide company. I have MCS and have called the manager about getting a Material Safety Data Sheet (MSDS) so I can tell what is making me sick. It took five months for the pesticide company to furnish me with these forms and then they called me and said they sent the wrong ones, that they no longer use that chemical, and they would send me the right ones. I haven't received them yet. What can I do? The store manager seems sympathetic but is new and isn't familiar with this ongoing problem.*

From a reader in Albuquerque, NM

A First, you should try to obtain the service tickets from the company for the last six months. If the manager can't find copies in his file, then he should call the pest control company and request copies. The service ticket must state what chemical was used, in what percentage, where it was applied, what pest it was applied to control, and the Environmental Protection Agency registration number of the pesticide. If any of those items are missing, then the pest control company is in violation of the law and the company should be reported to your local pesticide regulatory agency. Once you have the service ticket, you can request MSDS forms for any and all insecticides applied. If the pest control company is hesitant about furnishing you with the documents you request, then don't hesitate to call the regulatory agency.

I often state in this column that you should always ask for labels and MSDSs for any pesticides a pest control company plans on using. It is equally important, if not more so, that they give you a service ticket with all the information stated above when they complete the work. No matter how much or little pesticide they may use, it has to be documented. This includes places of business as well as homes, outdoor sprays as well as indoor sprays, and bait stations as well as liquid insecticides.

9

Home Remedies from Readers

I have asked readers to offer their own home remedies for pest control and have received many responses. Following are some of the pest control methods offered. I do not know which remedies work and which do not. Be careful when using some of the methods listed below as some of the products recommended, such as boric acid, are not entirely safe and should be used very carefully around children and pets.

Cockroaches

I read your column on Tuesdays about bugs. I have used your method of dish soap and Vaseline for ants and it works. The reason I am writing is to share a recipe for killing waterbugs (cockroaches):

> *4 tablespoons of boric acid*
> *2 tablespoons of flour*
> *1 tablespoon of cocoa*

I put the mixture in jar lids around areas where the roaches were and they disappeared. Have you heard of this recipe?

From a reader in Albuquerque, NM

Ants, Cockroaches, and Mice

First, let me say that we (the Chapel Hill News*) run your column every week. I always enjoy reading it because not only are you entertaining, but you're against pesticides. Here are my offerings for your book: If ants are coming in through doors or windows, put a cinnamon stick across the path. They will not cross it. And according to* *a Latino friend of mine, tile floors are too cold for cockroaches and mice. They don't like tile; therefore, it's a natural repellent.*

From a reader in Chapel Hill, NC

Gophers

Although the remedy I discovered is for gophers, not insects, I'd like to tell you about it anyway.

I discovered that you can get rid of gophers by pouring garlic salt down the hole. I don't know what happens on the gopher's end, but it works. No more activity at the hole and no new holes.

If you add a section to your book or column where you use this, you may use my name.

From Barbara Witterick in Santa Maria, CA

Cockroaches, Camel Crickets, and Ants

Thanks for your column. I have used with great success concoctions containing boric acid that I can buy at drugstores. Boric acid is good for roaches, camel crickets (the scourge of damp southern basements and storage areas), and ants. I mix the acid with various edible ingredients, once with hush puppy mix and a little water. For ants I use a little honey. Mix it with anything you know the insect likes.

For a one-shot insect killer, I keep a dilute solution of Joy [dishwashing soap] and water in a spray bottle in the kitchen. It's primarily used for light clean-up but it also kills some insects within a few minutes, including roaches. Try it, it's safe and cheap.

From a reader in Chapel Hill, NC

Ants

This is in response to your question about homemade solutions to get rid of pests. I use a syrup made out of corn syrup, honey, white sugar, and water. Put the mixture on the stove until the sugars melt and it's syrupy but pourable, and then add a good amount of boric acid powder. You can apply the syrup to the spots where ants congregate and on their trails. They love the sugars and run to get it, and then the boric acid gets them. I used this remedy this year a couple of times, and it totally wiped out the ant colony that was under my house and trying to get in. I had a bad infestation last year, and this year I had no problem because I used this stuff at the first sign of them. It's also a good solution because you can put it exactly where you want to without having to spread it around where it's not needed. The syrup formula isn't an exact one, either, just mix it all up until it looks good to you. The ants don't care about the proportions of the ingredients, they just like the sugar!

From a reader in Richmond, VA

Crickets, Cockroaches, and Ants

I was pleased to read your column in today's Atlantic City Press *regarding pesticides sprayed outdoors. Many folks in my neighborhood spray constantly and/or have a commercial service [do their spraying]. . . . When I tactfully mention that chemicals go right through our sandy soil and into Delaware Bay (and in my windows if I don't catch on and close them soon enough), they smile and laugh as if such a notion could only come from a wild woman! I guess I'm flabbergasted that they can't see it.*

The reason I'm writing, however, is to give you a couple of great remedies for crickets and perhaps roaches as well. Get a box of 20 Mule Team Borax and sprinkle generously around doorways and corners inside or outside. For ants, use boric acid, especially when you detect their trails. This works well in garages and sheds. Boric acid can be swept away and reapplied. While you wouldn't want to inhale it etc., it is not dangerous if it comes in contact with the skin.

I read once that cucumber peelings repel ants but that doesn't seem to slow my little visitors.

I applaud your efforts to help people see the light. I hope you are more successful than I am.

From Joy Black in North Cape May, NJ

Cockroaches and Fleas

Dear Richard Bugman,

When I lived in New York City, I was able to wipe out roach colonies in two apartments with the following method. This method is not to be used if pets are around.

Mix a couple of tablespoons of boric acid with water, until the consistency of cake frosting, and spread it on a slice of bread. (Any bread will do.) Place in the plastic lid from a coffee can, and trickle a little water over it until there's water visible all around the bread. Place one of these inside the (cold) oven or broiler, and another in a dark cabinet (under the sink is good). Every day or two, make sure there is still water around the bread in the plastic lid.

That's really all there is to it. Pretty soon, no more roaches.

Boric acid is wonderful stuff. If someone is doing renovation, a cou-ple handfuls of the stuff in an area soon to be closed off will keep the roaches away. Oh, yes, someone else wrote about fleas on pets. The best stuff is called Advantage—it's a small tube of liquid placed under the fur on the back of the cat or dog's neck once a month. It kills the fleas on the pet, and eventually all the fleas in the house. I only used it once this year, and never saw another sign of fleas.

Yes, we have plenty of bugs here . . .

From a reader in San Francisco, CA

Ants

Really do appreciate your environmentally sensitive approach to insect control, read here in Florida in the Stuart News.

There are devilish species of ants here, which truly can try one's patience. I refer to ghost, pharaoh, and crazy ants. They are so tiny that one can barely see them. However, in a full-fledged invasion, they're impossible to miss. I have had good results with the commercial baits that contain boric acid or Boraxo. My daughter, who lives on the west coast of Florida, has used her own recipe consisting of grape jelly and boric acid, which she has found to be very effective. My own observation is that these ants are par-tial to honey. I was totally unable to keep them away from the honey jar, which I used daily in my coffee. I finally prevailed, but it involved keeping the honey in the fridge, and giving up honey in my coffee. (So, who really prevailed?) I believe a honey/boric acid bait would be super effective, but so sticky and messy that it's probably not worth the effort.

However, my ace in the hole for many decades has been tal-cum powder. I don't remember how I learned of its value, or if it was serendipity. It appears that ants do not/cannot tolerate talc. For many years in our home on Long Island, New York, we would have a springtime invasion of small black ants in the kitchen through a crack between wall and floor. A timely and liberal appli-cation of talc in and around the crack would stem the tide—no more ants (until, perhaps, next spring).

Recently, here in Stuart, we had a invasion of little black ants from outdoors, which were then attracted to the commercial bait and ate it greedily. However, the number of ants kept increasing, and I was putting out more and more bait. I could see where they were coming in: up the front wall and then into the kitchen between the

135

closed window and its frame. What eventually stopped them was a generous application of talc on the inside and outside windowsills and at other points along the ant trail outside.

A subsequent invasion of the same type of ants involved an ant trail to the front doorjamb, then through a crack and through (inside) the walls, emerging through a crack in the kitchen—a favorite destination. Again, the bait seemed to be attracting more and more ants, so I resorted to talc, all around the doorjamb, and in the cracks in the kitchen (a separation between the counter and splashguard, and cracks where the splashguard and wall join). This required some perseverance, using a Q-tip to apply the powder in the cracks, as each time a path was blocked, those clever ants found a new point of entry. At last, though, they gave up.

I'm not sure why talcum powder is so effective, but I suspect it may act on these tiny critters like diatomaceous earth does on other, larger insects. Talc may not be totally innocuous, but I believe it's far less dangerous than the wholesale spraying of toxic chemicals that is going on here and elsewhere, or so it seems. In fact, the condo complex here is regularly treated with a type of time-release pesticide, which is spread on the soil around the outside of each building. This effort obviously does not keep ants (and other critters) out of our unit; I have to wonder if, in fact, it drives them in?

Also, I am an environmental educator (on leave of absence to care for my ailing dad). One of the aspects of the natural world that I really enjoyed exploring (with children or on my own) was insects and their allies—they are amazingly diverse, beautiful, fascinating, etc., not to mention the base of many, many food chains/webs/pyramids and invaluable as pollinators of so many plants (including many of our food crops). Therefore, I am extremely ambivalent when it comes to destroying these critters, but would rather not share my living quarters with most of them. Thanks for sharing your knowledge.

From Joan Schmidt in Stuart, FL

Ants

I mix one part sugar to four parts of borax (commonly used for laundry). I sprinkle this on anthills. The ants eat both the sugar and the borax—I suppose they can't tell which is which. The ants disappear in a few days. Do this, of course, in dry weather.

From Martha Boyce in Tucson, AZ

Multiple Pests

We want to share our personal success story with you regarding pest control. When we first moved into our home twenty-plus years ago, we had problems with black widow spiders, cockroaches, silverfish, and crickets seasonally, so for a year we had a pest control service spray monthly, then we did the do-it-yourself pest control for a few years. We never conquered the problems. What did work out beautifully is that when we stopped spraying chemicals in the house and yard, geckos propagated and we no longer have pests. I watch the geckos at night on our windows nailing moths that land where there is light, and am in total awe of nature and very grateful.

From Holly in Arizona

Ants and Crickets

I have had excellent results with ant and cricket elimination by using boiling water. Heat on stove until boiling, and pour water down ant holes. Hook hose to hot water tank to spray along home outside walls for crickets.

From R. E. Gentry in Richmond, VA

Multiple Pests

We have been coming to Tucson for the winters (September through April–May). Upon leaving our place in the care of home care businesses, we were told to leave fresh leaves of basil in the corners of the inside walls and behind furniture. In all the months and years (since 1990) we have been doing this, we haven't had any problems with insect infestation. We live in the southwest area outside of Tucson.

From a reader in Tucson, AZ

Ants

I read your article and would like to share my home remedy to controlling ants.

I put bay leaves and Listerine mouthwash in the corners of my food pantry to prevent little ants getting into my flour and powdered sugar. This remedy helps a lot and I will always use this since it works wonders!

I would like to mention a homemade remedy that I have used on hummingbird feeders to keep those nasty ants away. I wipe the string that holds the hummingbird feeder with Vaseline petroleum jelly. I have been using this remedy for a long time and it really knocks those ants down.

Another remedy I would like to mention is that I wipe my houseplants' leaves with olive oil and this destroys those little flying bugs that like the moisture around the leaves.

One remedy for roaches that I forgot to mention is to place bowls around the house filled with boric acid. It also works wonders for creepy crawlers!

Thank you very much for allowing me to share some home remedies for your articles and your book.

From Anna Victoria Reich in Albuquerque, NM

Ants

Since I'm an Avon rep, I'm not really supposed to reveal this cure for ants, but the company's Skin-So-Soft Bath Oil works better than anything I've ever tried. Just spray some where the ants are coming in and they leave—it's nontoxic and also smells good (to humans).

From a reader in San Francisco, CA

Cockroaches

I enjoy your column immensely. I usually clip it out and send it to my sister in West Virginia. She has reactions to most chemicals and never uses sprays or any chemicals around her house.

I am also very sensitive to chemicals and never spray around my home either. I clean with vinegar and water or baking soda and water. If I need a cleaner I use Bon Ami.

The best thing I've ever used for roaches is slices of raw cucumber placed in the cupboards and kitchen drawers. Replace them when they dry out.

I don't even use diatomaceous earth outside because I'm not sure how it will affect the geckos, lizards, and toads in my yard (I also don't have any cats, who would kill them), and all of the above help keep the insect population under control.

From a reader in Tucson, AZ

Yellow Jackets and Fruit Flies

In response to your request for insect-control home remedies: Several years ago, after my neighbor had complained many times about yellow jackets, I bought both of us a bee/wasp trap from the sale pages of the Garden of Eden catalog. I'm sure you have seen them as they *are copies of an old design—molded in glass, with feet, an opening at the top (with cork) and one in the bottom surrounded by a moat that contains a liquid. There is a wire around the neck for hanging. The next year yellow jackets were not a problem, but fruit flies were, so I filled the trap's moat with malt vinegar and hung in from a cupboard under a kitchen cabinet.* Bingo! *It's the only thing that has controlled these pests for me and it's nontoxic. Fruit flies flock to it. One evening this summer I had to dump the malt vinegar three times.*

From Jane in Richmond, VA

Ants

Years ago I read Rachel Carson's Silent Spring *and Jacques Cousteau's* Calypso *newsletter and both of them scared me so much that I never used a chemical spray again.*

My garden contains buttercups, birds (robins, finches, sparrows, jays, hummingbirds, orioles, and a variant here and there), and squirrels; a frog and a salamander have appeared a couple of times. Of course, ants have their own way of doing things and they want to come into the house. This is a "no-no." I have found that a spray consisting of about $1/2$ cup of water and a few hefty squirts of Tabasco sauce works. Spray liberally in their entrance; spray a cloth with the mixture and wipe the pathway they have used. They tap dance right out of the house.

I also have a hummingbird feeder outside and of course the ants love the water as much as the birds do. I soak a Q-tip with Mongolian fire oil and put as much of the oil on the wire holding the feeder as I can; the ants do not like it.

These treatments can last from indefinitely to a short period, but they are a much better way than using pesticides. Thank you for your column.

From a reader in Oakland, CA

Cockroaches

Years ago, when I lived in Honolulu, I accidentally discovered a method to be rid of cockroaches. Our home was on a cement slab. One night we entertained guests at dinner. Later, we adjourned to the living room, with the last of the red wine. To my horror, a big cockroach encroached upon my goblet, crawled inside, and drowned. Fortunately, our guests were spared.

Thereafter, I bought cheap red wine to put in tumblers that I placed strategically in the house. Several days and several drowned cockroaches later, they got the message and stayed outside where they belong.

I don't know why the cockroaches were attracted to the red wine. I haven't had a problem at my current residence.

My difficulty now is with spiders. Thanks again for your interesting, informative column.

From a reader in Alameda, CA

Multiple Pests

Dear Bugman,

Just discovered your column in the San Francisco Chronicle. *Great! It reminded me of something that happened long ago in Tucson, Arizona. My wife and I were living way out in the desert. At night we would like to sit in front of our trailer and converse under the stars and the moon. However, the multitude of insects there would get on our nerves. What we did was take a hooded light, like the ones that mechanics use to work on cars, and lower it down to within about an inch and a half to two inches off the ground. This let enough light out so we could see where we were walking, without getting in our eyes, or distracting us too much from the moon and stars. Another thing it did was attract the insects to the light. Ants would set up a perimeter around the light and grab the insects that would fly down to try to get to the light. This was fascinating, effective, and required no pesticides.*

From a reader in Oakland, CA

Ants

This is not exactly "homemade," but it's so easy that I thought you might be interested.

For ants (that are visible) simply grab your spray bottle of Glass Plus (glass and surface cleaner) and instantly zap them. Then wipe up with paper towel. In my previous house, each spring I had a steady, long line of ants marching along a wall (where there was a window) and then onto my kitchen counter. They literally stopped dead in their tracks when I sprayed with the Glass Plus. A huge colony of them also decided to take up residence in my curbside mailbox. Again, they got a spray attack and folded up their tents, you might say. And they did not return either.

From Sally Goodfellow in Midlothian, VA

❧ **The following home remedies were sent to me by fellow entomologists when I solicited their responses on the Entomologist List server.**

Cockroaches

I have had success keeping roaches out of kitchen and bathroom cupboards by sprinkling fresh or dried catnip on the cupboard floors.

Fleas

As you requested, here's a home remedy for fleas that works like a charm, because my mother used it once many years ago (before growth-inhibitor sprays) when her house got positively overrun with fleas after keeping my sister's Siamese cat for a while. They were in the closets, where the cat liked to sleep, under the bed, the living room, sofa cushions, etc. She had heard that black walnut leaves repel fleas so she got a bunch of fresh black walnut leaves and laid them everywhere the fleas were. In a week or so, there were truly no more fleas! We were all amazed, as those old "home remedies" don't always work that well, but this sure did. She never had another problem with them, either. I have since wondered if the leaves must be fresh (the volatile oils, perhaps) or if you could dry and powder them and use them as a dust for under chair cushions, etc. I certainly wouldn't use it directly on a cat or dog, though. I do know that black walnut roots contain some sort of toxin that inhibits many other plants from growing around or under the trees, so maybe this has something to do with it. All I know is that it works!

Ants

I worked in a lab where fire ants were raised. We used a coating of baby powder on our rubber boots when digging up mounds as well as on the insides of some containers. The ants seemed to have no actual aversion to it, but it makes an antproof barrier on smooth vertical surfaces because the ants get no traction. This may be why the baby powder remedy works in some situations.

10

Least Favorite Bugs

🕷 I wrote a column asking readers to let me know what their least favorite bug was and why. I received many responses, including a letter from an entire third-grade class. The readers could use any criteria they wished for making their choice, such as: What bug would you least like to see crawling across your living room floor? What bug would you least like to share a phone booth with? Here are some of the responses to the question.

Daddy Longlegs

Forty-some years ago, when I was eight years old, my mother died (causes unrelated to daddy longlegs!). When at Girl Scout camp that summer, our group laid our sleeping bags in a grove of pines, then went to a clearing to study constellations. When we returned—by flashlight—thousands and thousands of daddy longlegs were running across our sleeping bags. Tried to get to sleep, but every time I heard a pine tag fall during the night, I knew it was really a daddy longlegs that would fall on me. In spite of understanding the origin of my phobia, my heart nearly stops when I see them (apparently I had always played with them prior to that night). I've tried learning about them, these blind harvestmen, in hopes of waylaying the phobia, but without much avail. It's stupid, I know. . . . (And they most certainly do bite.) P.S.: I enjoy your column.

Cockroaches

You're kidding, right? You want to know everyone's least favorite bug?! That's easy, and I already know which one is going to win hands (or is that pinchers?) down: the cockroach (any variety— German, Japanese).

Ants are cute, industrious little critters: They work hard and raise little mushroom gardens and do cute stuff. Ladybugs are

pretty and are said to bring good luck. Caterpillars turn into beau-
tiful butterflies. Spiders are helpful because they eat flies.

But cockroaches have absolutely no redeeming social value.
They aren't attractive, they don't bring good luck, they don't turn
into something pretty, and the damn things are almost impossible
to kill. Roaches can live on a spot of grease (and Lord knows I'm not
a perfect housekeeper), but that fact alone is enough to drag out the
disinfectant. Roaches are said to be able to survive a nuclear explo-
sion. I even read (although I have not personally tried this) that if
you cut off a roach's head, it can still live 11 days (bet Marie
Antoinette could have used that little trick). What's more, which
would you least rather have crawling (or flying?) across your floor
if you had a houseful of dinner guests whom you really wanted to
impress: ant, ladybug, caterpillar, or cockroach? I am truly blessed
to live in a house that (I hope) is roach free. However, years ago,
when I first got married, my husband and I spent a year in the Navy
at Kingsville, Texas. It really is true that things are bigger in Texas,
and I swear, we had a cockroach in our apartment that took up half
the bathroom. The roach, needless to say, got first turn in the bath-
room. One night, my husband came home to find me standing on
the toilet screaming, cornered by "The Roach." Despite numerous
and plentiful applications of boric acid powder, the roach never went
away, and as far as I know still lives there happily to this day.

Miller Moths

I hate miller moths! They're so fluttery and ugly and remind me of
little bats. I've hated them since I was a little girl, and now I'm in
my forties. I sure wouldn't stay in any phone booth for long if there
was one in there! Every spring and summer here in Colorado we get
them by the thousands; which I've learned is because they're migrat-
ing to the mountains. I wish they'd just keep going . . .

My husband laughs at me and gets annoyed with me and my
fear. Is there anything they don't like that I might use around the
house to discourage them from hanging around? Our cats are good
little hunters of [miller moths], but I'd rather they didn't get inside
in the first place! Thank you. Mary—Aurora, CO

Crickets

Lots of people think this bug I abhor is "cute." Oh, Jiminy! Well,
we can thank Pinocchio for that. And countless other folks, mostly

city dwellers, believe this insect's "music" epitomizes the good country life. But I, who have lost so much sleep to the critter's shenanigans, would rather see a roach, a hornet, or a wild African boar skitter across my floor than a cricket.

Crickets chew raggedy holes in clothes in a laundry basket. They nibble the edges of rugs. They have inhabited my cedar plank ceiling and made so much noise up there I would not hear the Concorde break the sound barrier directly over my house, let alone catch a single note of my loudest soundtrack.

A cricket in the TV room is an especially profound annoyance, especially a cricket who produces that one incessant singularly piercing shriek that makes a Cape Kennedy blast-off seem like a whisper.

Furthermore, a cricket anywhere in the house is next to impossible to find. Lift the couch, shift the TV, rip up the wall-to-wall carpet, the cricket is nowhere to be found—but his "song" wails on in your ear like the truly wretched Walkman from Hell.

Worst of all, should you finally, after hours of maniacal searching, discover his hiding place and actually see the screeching destroyer of your sanity, he will leap up to your full height and lodge himself loudly in your hair.

I do not like crickets, I do not like them at all!

Spiders

About six years ago, my then-fiancé witnessed my reaction to a spider actually on me. It took half an hour to calm me down. He used to think my spider phobia was funny until the day he proposed using a pop-up spider book that had an 8" tarantula wearing the engagement ring. Now, my husband is happy to remove the spiders from inside the house. I don't care how—dead or alive. I know that spiders eat other bugs, and I don't like other bugs in the house, either. But I just can't tolerate spiders, unless they're outside.

Cockroaches

I am answering your request to send the name of my least favorite bug. It is the cockroach. I associate it with filth and a carrier of disease. I await your results.

From a reader in Bloomington, IN

Ants

My least favorite bug is the ant. They . . . crawl into my hum-

mingbird feeders and live off the sugar in the feeders. They are pests! I try to prevent the ants from going into the hummingbird feeders by rubbing petroleum jelly on the branches and placing sachets of lavender in sacks so the sack scares the ants away.

Fleas

The flea! *The agony and grief that fleas cause is just awful. Not to mention all the money I've spent over the years–exterminators, over-the-counter products (don't work), veterinarian costs, and carpet cleaning (doesn't work).*

This summer is especially bad here in South Jersey. Any advice and remedies you can offer will be most appreciated.

Thank you in advance for your help. I read your column every Sunday.

Potato Bugs

A potato bug—no contest!!

Crickets, Bold-Faced Hornets and Yellow Jackets

I am not at all bothered by bugs, but if I were to find one I hate the most and why, it's got to be the cricket—those noisy, black little bugs that keep me up at night with their music. My wife loves their song; not me. The cricket is the one for in the house. Now, if I were in a telephone booth, and I were trapped with a nest of bold-faced hornets or yellow jackets, this would cause my heart to race. All other bugs I can get away from, if I need or want to. Not those hornets or yellow jackets. Know what I mean? My wife and I very much enjoy your column in the Richmond Times Dispatch. *We're in the northern neck of Virginia.*

Cockroaches and Stinkbugs

Just want to contribute my vote for all-time worst bugs. Unfortunately, my choice will probably outlive us all. Anything that even remotely resembles a cockroach gives me the heebie jeebies. I reach for the Raid because I can't stand that crunchy sound they make when you stomp them.

I grew up in Georgia and we had huge flying "roaches." I believe they were actually palmetto bugs. They were especially abundant in my elementary school (behind any closed door!) and on my college campus. Now that I live in Richmond, Virginia, we have small, brown, roach-looking creatures. They are not quite as bad, but I rarely let them live when I see them. And you can be guaranteed that anything bigger than my pinkie nail will die if I see it!

Lately, my close second has been these little bugs we used to call stinkbugs or pincher bugs. They are brown, about 1/2" long and skinny with little pinchers in front. I don't mind them hiding under rocks outside, but lately they've been inviting themselves in for tea. They die too. Thanks for a useful column!

Spiders

Spiders, no question about it. I have a severe arachnophobia, probably having to do with the fact that growing up in north Denver, my bedroom was in the basement (the spiders love basements, you know). I'm from Aurora, CO.

Yellow Jackets and Cockroaches

I enjoyed your column asking for least favorite bugs. Mmmm . . . let's see. I don't like wasps or bumblebees, and I hate yellow jackets. Yellow jackets would top the list of insects I most do not want to be stuck with in a telephone booth (or any other enclosed space). But the worst bug, the bug I detest more than any other, the bug that ought to be eradicated from the earth is the roach. Any roach. Especially the wood roach, which I tend to see in my older home fairly frequently. At about 2 inches long, those things are nightmare bugs. They are nasty and ugly and just won't die when I smack them with a shoe, until I just pound the crap out of them. They show up in the bathroom and in the den. I hate them and the mess they make when I pound them to bits. They are filthy and nasty. So, the roach is my least favorite bug. Yuck.

From a reader in Decatur, AL

Deer Ticks

My least favorite bug is the deer tick because it carries Lyme Disease.

Children's Least Favorites

🕷 **A teacher discussed the subject with her third-grade class and had the students write down what their least favorite** bug was and why. She then kindly sent me a letter with the responses that are so outstanding that I have to share them. The students are from Hubert Humphrey Elementary School in Albuquerque, New Mexico.

"The bug I hate the most is the tarantula. I hate the tarantula because of all the movies that I have seen about tarantulas. They are very freaky. They seem poisonous and they look scary. They are very, very hairy. I really hate them. I'm afraid of them so much even though I'm a boy. I think some tarantulas could kill some-one. I hope I don't see a tarantula."

Elliot

"The bug I hate is a cockroach because they are ugly, creepy, wig-gly, and scary. When you squash them it makes an icky sound. The last time I saw one, I squished it and I threw mud at it and guts came out. I hate them and I run away from them."

Emmelisa

"My least favorite bug is a centipede because one time I was walk-ing in the garage when I saw a centipede and he crawled into my bathroom. My mom told my sister to get a butter knife and she did. My mom said to chop it in half so my sister said 'no.' So my mom did and it still was crawling so my mom turned on the water and it went down the drain. That's why I don't like centipedes."

Brittany K.

"I hate centipedes because one got in my house. My mom hit it with a frying pan. Once I found one in our garage."

Brittany H.

"The bug that freaks me out is the red spider because one time my mom asked me to go out back with her to spray bug spray and then there was a big red spider who was on our neighbor's cactus. My mom started spraying him with bug spray. She said, 'a long, slow death.' Then it started climbing the wall. She said 'gimme your shoe.' So I gave her my shoe and she killed him and that's why I don't like red spiders."

Brittney B.

"My worst enemy is a fly because they bug me. It makes me kill the fly and I hate houseflies very, very much."

Tate

"The bug I hate is cockroaches because they are creepy, ugly, and scary, and when you step on them they make a crunchy sound. The last time I saw a cockroach, I was scared. Then it hissed at me. I hate cockroaches."

Lindsy

"The bug I really hate is a cockroach because when I was getting my friend's scooter out of her garage to play with, I stepped on one. I was barefooted too. Now every time I see one I scream."

Cassidy

"I like ladybugs and some other bugs. I don't like black widows and cockroaches. They freak me out. Are cockroaches good or bad?"

Jordan

"I hate centipedes and I hate every bug in the world because they are scary and creepy, spiders too. I hate every bug."

Christina

"My least favorite bug is the tarantula because they could really hurt you and whenever I see one I shiver and I just walk right past them. They scare me. They're all furry, too. I just don't like them. I don't know why, I don't like them."

Drew

"I hate, hate, hate scorpions. They look deadly and scary. When they pop up their tail, I would run 100,000,000 miles and that is why I hate, hate, hate scorpions."

Bryce

"I like all bugs. They are very neat and they have a lot of energy. That is why I like bugs. I hate lice because they make you itch a lot. They are creepy. I heard about them in a panda movie. That is why I hate lice."

Alex S.

"I like ladybugs and praying mantis. I do not like cockroaches (especially the German type). I don't like black widows or scorpions. Not all spiders freak me out but centipedes do."

Laurel

"I think every bug is cool because it feels all weird when it crawls up you and looks awesome. The sound they make is weird."

Ryan

"I do not like black widows because they are creepy. Me and my sister were digging in the backyard and I asked my sister for a little shovel but she said no. So I played without the shovel. In five minutes we started fighting so then I got it. When I got it, I saw a spider on my leg and freaked out. My dad got it off. Before he got if off, it bit me. He noticed it was a male black widow."

Manda

"The scariest thing is a scorpion because it has a poison tail. I don't want to get bitten or stung by one."

Mark

"The bug that freaks me out is a ladybug. When they fly on me it scares me. When I move my hand the ladybug flies away. It freaks me out."

Laura

11

Special Letters and Comments

🐛 This section contains several letters on different subjects I received from the readers of my column. The first two are from folks who hold different religious points of view and both take me to task for things I have written. The following series of letters are responses I received after writing about fly-repellent water bags. These are followed by a couple of letters that don't fit anywhere else in the book.

🐛 I received this letter after publishing a column on sow bugs. My response to the writer and his response to my response follow.

Q *Your article about sow bugs was very interesting. You did write something that I must take you to task on, however. This was that sow bugs adapted to life on land. Your implication is that evolution is correct, when in fact no portion of evolution has ever been proven. Evolution is . . . the most ridiculous theory ever brought forward by anyone. It makes no sense whatsoever to anyone with even half a brain. Sow bugs were . . . created by God along with all other forms of life on this earth. Think about it, I mean really mull it over in your brain apart from what you have been taught, and you would agree that evolution is pure asininity. Don't be biased by what has been taught to you; think for yourself. If at the end of your deep pondering you still can say that all life descended from a one-cell animal, if you can still say that we are an accidental happening, then let me pose a question. The question is this: If in fact creation was the end result of some haphazard event following the big bang that scientists like to talk about, then where did that original material come from that caused the big bang? Remember that nothing can come from nothing. Something, someone, created that first gaseous material, and that someone was God; you can't get away from that fact.*

Thanks for your time, I await your answer.

From a reader in Powhatan, VA

A You are partially right. I believe God did create the universe with one big bang (energy) billions of years ago and everything has evolved and will evolve until the universe collapses back on itself. Then there will be another "big bang" and the process will start over again.

I am a deist in that I wholeheartedly believe that God created everything and all of the natural laws. After that, it was up to us (and evolution). I don't believe He interferes in our lives anymore, other than in our hearts and minds.

Reader's response

If you are right, then we will both pass into oblivion some day. If however I am correct, then I will spend eternity in heaven, while you are suffering in the Lake of Fire. Either way I have nothing to lose. You, however, may lose your soul. The difference between Jesus and the others is that Jesus was God come to earth in human form to die for our redemption. Not only that, but Jesus conquered death and the grave and rose again.

I really don't believe that you really thought it through before answering my admonition to think for yourself. Otherwise you wouldn't have answered my email so quickly.

I say where is the proof of evolution? Where is the missing link? There isn't one and none will ever be found because it never was. Each species reproduces only it's own kind. There is no evidence that any animal ever changed into another. A fruit fly is still a fruit fly after millions of generations. They have produced various coloration differences but the fruit fly remains a fruit fly. Scientists have never been able to change a fruit fly into any other type of fly, let alone change it into a mosquito, or a bee. As you know the fruit fly has the fastest rate of reproduction. Question: What happened when the first amphibian changed into a reptile? [W]hat did it mate with? Or did it happen that two amphibians changed at the same time[?] Still doesn't make any sense at all. Only Genesis makes sense to me.

. . . Watch [the Creation Network] sometime as they explain scientifically what really happened when God created the universe.

I am praying for you that the God that you believe in will reveal Himself to you in a special way. I have enjoyed "talking" with you and wish you the best. Keep the columns coming. Thank you.

The following exchange is from a very nice person in California who took exception to my suggesting that any pest should be killed.

Q *Hello and Happy Summer,*

It is cruel to encourage people to complain about, deter, and kill creatures. All creatures have a right to exist and thrive wherever they are. People benefit from education about creatures that help them enjoy, respect, and appreciate them from a distance and encouragement to be at peace in their immediate environment. It is wrong to kill creatures for any reason; it is important to teach people to make the best of whatever happens. When we promote the lives of creatures, we are promoting our own lives! Creatures are not "pets" for humans.

Thank you for your kind interest. Buddhist chant for true happiness: "Nam-Myoho-Renge-Kyo."

From a reader in San Francisco, CA

A I can't disagree with most of what you say. I never encourage anyone to indiscriminately kill anything. Having said that, I do not believe anyone wants to share their home with termites or their clothing with clothes moths or their food with ants or roaches. This is not a perfect world and occasionally the "creatures" and humans interact with each other and sometimes someone has to go. I do stress that when dealing with "pests," that we limit our control mechanisms to methods that will only affect the pest and not kill nontarget insects. I don't kill anything in my home, but on campus, where I am responsible for the peace of mind, concerning bugs, of over 20,000 people, I have to eliminate nuisance insects for the betterment of the campus community.

You are absolutely right when you say we should observe, study, and learn from our smaller neighbors. Public education about insects, pests, pesticides, and so on is the most important aspect of any integrated pest management program and is the reason why I write this column and why I frequently appear on TV and the radio, give lectures, and conduct training seminars.

Thank you for your eloquent and provocative letter.

🦗 **The letter below is from the PETA organization (People for the Ethical Treatment of Animals), and was written in response to an answer I gave to a flea problem.**

Thank you for printing People for the Ethical Treatment of Animals' (PETA's) tips for fighting fleas without toxins in your "Ask the Bugman" column. PETA also has suggestions for kindly controlling cockroaches, which we hope you will share with your readers.

Many people might wonder why they shouldn't reach for the Raid when a cockroach clan moves in. For starters, insects can feel pain. At a symposium at the Zoological Society in London earlier this year, Dr. Chris Sherwin of the University of Bristol noted that the criteria researchers use to assess the mental states of vertebrates often produce similar results among insects. Added Dr. Stephen Wickens, "People who think insects don't feel any pain may be wrong. Perhaps people should think twice before reaching for the fly spray."

Insects, including cockroaches, are also fascinating beings once you get to know them. For example, cockroaches smell with their mouths and with the long antennae—which contain 40,000 nerve endings—on the tops of their heads. They have "ears" on their rears—two little hairs called cerci that detect vibrations— and compound eyes made up of 2,000 individual lenses (human eyes have only one lens).

Even if readers aren't ready to roll out the welcome mat, roaches, like all animals, deserve to be treated with respect. There are many simple, common-sense steps people can take to encourage cockroaches to move out without resorting to mortal methods:

* *Don't provide roaches with food or water. Don't let dirty dishes stack up in the sink, store food in tightly sealed containers, and keep trash in bins with tight-fitting lids. Dry up roaches' water supply by fixing dripping faucets and other leaks, and be careful not to overwater houseplants (soggy soil is a cockroach's favorite cocktail).*

- *If you see roaches, scatter whole bay leaves throughout your house, including inside kitchen cabinets. To roaches, bay leaves smell worse than dirty socks! Catnip works, too. According to Iowa State University scientists, catnip is 100 times more effective at repelling roaches than DEET is.*
- *Remove roaches' hiding places. Keep compost heaps as far from your house as possible, always wash out food containers before storing them for recycling, and don't let them or old newspapers pile up.*
- *Prevent roaches from entering your home in the first place by sealing up holes and cracks. Baby roaches can squeeze into a space as thin as a dime.*
- *Even when it comes to roaches, PETA thinks the best policy is always "live and let live."*

    Sincerely,

Paula Moore
Staff Writer
PETA
501 Front St.
Norfolk, VA 23510
Tel.: 757–622–7382, ext. 312

🦗 **I wrote a column about using zip-lock bags half filled with water to prevent flies from entering a structure. Below is the letter and some of the replies I received.**

Q *How can I keep flies out of my home without using pesticides?*
From a reader in Albuquerque, NM

A It is not known why or how this works but it is worth a try. You can tape sandwich-size zip-lock bags half filled with water to your doors. These water bags will repel flies. Perhaps the reflections in the water make a difference, somehow scaring or confusing the flies. Entomologists know that flies are phototropic, meaning they are attracted to light, but they don't know why these water bags repel flies.

    "I have no earthly idea," said an entomologist from

Iowa State University, when asked how this works. He was extremely curious to know whether it really works or not. If it does work, you could tape water bags to doors everywhere—and on your horse barn, livestock yard, and poultry house, as well.

If you want to try this, here are some guidelines: Use a sandwich-sized zip-lock bag. Fill it about half full with water. If it's completely full, then it doesn't move and it apparently is important for the bag to move around a little. Tape the top of the bag to the outside of your door. Replenish the water as needed.

You may get some questions as to why you have little bags of water taped to your door. Here are some explanations you can use:

- It attracts flies.
- It scares flies.
- If it freezes, we know it's cold outside.
- If it's boiling, we know it's hot outside.
- To see if anyone is paying attention.
- I don't know, ask the Bugman. This is his idea.

When you drive around the city look for zip-lock water bags on doors. If you see them, you will know the homeowner read the column as you couldn't possibly get this sort of information anywhere else. If anyone tries this I would be very interested in the results, as would the rest of the readers who may not be inclined to tape water-filled baggies to their doors.

Responses

I had to write to share the success and the comments on your fly-repellent water bag. I hate to stop what I am doing to let the dog out and in, so we just keep the kitchen door open for him. Needless to say, my kitchen and all its smells attract many flies. I have two fly swatters on hand and sometimes murder fifteen or so a day. On the day I read your silly solution, I promptly went into the kitchen, killed all the flies there within, and hung a water bag in the doorway. Not only did no more flies enter, but also we were fly free for days. I couldn't really believe it, so I put it to a test. I boiled five pounds of chicken and let it set on the counter to cool (usually a big fly attractant). To my amazement not one fly entered through the kitchen door. Since your article on August 10, I have had maybe five flies in the kitchen (and they might have come in through different entryways).

Most people who comment are very skeptical but impressed when I convince them that it really worked for us. Now I will try them at the farm where I work. I wish I could hang them from the horses.

From a reader in Martinez, CA

Read your column and wanted to share that I saw a similar thing in Nova Scotia. My husband and I were visiting up there last month and noted small paper bags blown up with air, tied at the top, and taped to the top corners of entry doors. We first noticed it as we entered the visitor's center in Baddeck, Cape Breton Island. We were told it was there to discourage flies from entering the building. We then noticed this interesting paper-bag décor a few other times during our week-long stay in Nova Scotia. Kind of blows the reflecting water theory. I must say there were not any pesky flies in the room, and up there the flies are black flies—I am still healing from some of the bites I got while there. Very interesting story!

Hey Bugman, just wanted to tell you that we were getting a lot of flies in the house, so we did as you suggested and put a plastic bag with water hanging from our door and we have only had one or two flies in the past week. Thanks for the tip!!

Enjoyed your article on flies and water bags that appeared in our local paper. The interesting thing is that I recently returned from a trip to Cozumel, Mexico. The resort we stayed at had bags of water all over the eating areas. Never having seen this, I asked why. The answers all related to keeping flies away but nobody was able to give me a reasonable answer as to how. Some people said the bag was filled with vinegar and water and this seeped through the pores in the plastic (?).

The effectiveness of these bags varied. If we had a breeze it worked.

If there was no breeze, it didn't. No matter, as it was an interesting concept and allowed for a lot of discussion.

Saw your article on water bags to keep flies away. I saw this done in Fiji at an outdoor restaurant with one on each pole. No flies. I've told this to many people and no one takes me seriously. I use one on my back porch.

Read your article last week in the SF Chronicle *or* Examiner. *I swear, the bags work. We were having a problem with flies coming in from the deck (we have a puppy who does his business out there, and we must leave the door slightly open). Immediately, there was a huge improvement. I admit I was skeptical. It hasn't kept out every single fly, but has helped cut the population by at least 90 percent. Also put one by the living room window downstairs, huge improvement there also, which is nice, because in San Francisco, I don't have any screens on my windows and we keep the windows cracked open for ventilation year round.*

. . . [W]ater bags hang above the windows and doors of the LaConner Tavern (LaConner, Washington), our favorite Northwest spot for fish and chips. The waitpersons say they're for the flies or so that tourists will ask. By the way, Tom Robbins (Even Cowgirls Get the Blues) *lives in LaConner and is frequently seen in the tavern.*

It works! It works! I placed a zip-lock plastic bag two-thirds full of water [on top of my trash can] and no flies. . . . Thanks.
From a reader in South Jersey, NJ

While we haven't used this technique in our own backyard to keep the flies away, my wife and I saw it work quite well while in Spain on our honeymoon.
Our tour bus stopped at a roadside cantina for lunch. It had an outdoor area filled with tables. On each table were open dishes of several salsas, tortilla chips, pickled vegetables and other "exposed" condiments. Also, the kitchen area was open to the outdoors.

The bags you describe in your 10/6 Sun-Times *article were hanging on a clothesline over the entire cafe. Neither my wife nor I had any idea what these water bags were about. When we asked we were given the explanation you write about.*

Indeed, there were no flies, or any other bothersome insects for that matter, to vex our lunch hour. On our way back to the bus, however, we noticed lots and lots of flies and other insects just outside the restaurant and in the parking areas. It seemed like a crazy idea, but it also seemed to work.

From a reader in Mt. Prospect, IL

This method of fly and wasp repellent does work. I was on vacation in Mexico and our group decided to go horseback riding. Mind you, we stayed at a five-star hotel, and the bar area on the beach was being bombarded with flies and wasps. This horse ranch had an area where the guests waited outside. I noticed half-filled plastic bags of water, tied to and hanging every few feet from the beams of this 20 x 20 canopied waiting area. The manager said that's what keeps the bugs away. There were no flies or wasps in this particular area. I tried this as soon as I returned home on my back porch in August, in the city of Chicago, on the south side. Flies and hornets did not come near my porch.

From a reader in Chicago, IL

*Your article regarding the use of bags of water to repel insects appeared in our paper today (*Jackson Sun, *Jackson, Tennessee). I just had to write and add this bit of verification.*

This past July, while traveling in Nicaragua, I stayed at a place where the dining tables were on an open-air porch. Above each table a bag of water was suspended by string from the ceiling. These bags were a little larger than the ones you described. In "baggie equivalents" they were probably about a half-gallon size. Of course, we gringos amused ourselves by setting them into a swinging motion at every meal. Someone speculated that the urge to swing them was so irresistible that this was, indeed, their secret to repelling success, with the movement being the repelling factor. We also heard that the water greatly magnified the insects' own reflections, thus frightening them away. I would be interested to learn the solution to this mystery when you discover it.

From a reader in Jackson, TN

🐂 The following letter is from a reader who was leaving the area after reading my column in the *Albuquerque Tribune.*

Dear Mr. Fagerlund,

You would not believe what I've been going through with your beloved bugs of all kinds, even though they may be species that are not bugs but some other life form that was destined to save the world until I intervened.

I would stay out of their life if they would stay out of mine! *Why must they mess around with my toothbrushes and other possessions? Do they have to sleep in my bed, when surely they could find bedding elsewhere? Believe me, it'll be a helluva long time before I kiss up to some specimen.*

The vinegar seemed to work but there would be legions more marching onward. But for sure, anything *is preferred to spiders, roaches, flies, and wasps.*

I'll miss your column (but not that much). I'm off to Maine in mid-October for help from my kids to hold me together. I'll have the mosquitoes to cope with. Well, if they are bad, I'll raise a glass to you! Your descriptions were interesting. Finally had my annual praying mantis two days ago.

From a reader in Albuquerque, NM

I didn't tell her that she can run but she can't hide. My column is also distributed in Maine.

12

True Stories

🐜 **The following anecdotes are all true. With over thirty years in the bug business, I have met many interesting folks and bugs (and other animals), and have learned from many human–bug encounters to really appreciate life. The first story is about Katy Maddox, one of the most interesting people I have never met. I have known Katy now for a few years but have never met her. We communicate solely through email.**

The Katy Maddox Chronicles

I received my first email from Katy on 17 March 1999. The first letter appears below. We corresponded many times throughout the year trying to solve her problem. Katy lives in an apartment in New York City and found an article I wrote on bed bugs in the *Daily Lobo,* the campus newspaper for the University of New Mexico, which was posted on the Internet.

When we solved the bed bug problem, Katy developed minor bug problems that we tried to solve as they came up. Subsequently, we developed an online friendship that has transcended bugs.

I still have nightmares about the bugs that tortured me relentlessly for six months. There are moments of panic—I feel myself getting sweaty and my stomach tightens with fear and dread—when I think they may be back. I wake up to find a small, itchy bump on my ankle: a bug bite. At these moments, my mind races as I envision the coming days, weeks, months. Quick, find a plastic mattress cover! Call the exterminators! Buy twenty cases of Skin-So-Soft! In

---

the meantime, cruise the real-estate listings in the paper. . . . I am on constant alert, ready to spring into action should the enemy infiltrate my mattress and my life again. Gone are the days when I looked upon bugs as harmless, mildly annoying creatures; now I see only blood-sucking parasites who would like nothing more than to drag me down into their hellish pit of pestilence.

Katy Maddox

✿⃕ Katy Maddox is a bug-phobic aspiring writer living in New York.

After reading your piece on bed bugs in the online version of the Lobo *paper, I felt I had to email you. You see, something has been eating me alive each night in my sleep for the last month or so. For the life of me, I couldn't find a bug, nor traces of a bug. I called three exterminators, an entomologist, went to two dermatologists, and did major research on the web. I was told all sorts of conflicting things (like, "You can't have bed bugs if you don't see any blood on your sheets," and "Bed bugs are as big as ladybugs, you'd know if you had them," and "Real bed bug cases are quite rare," but then "They can be quite small and hide anywhere, you could have no idea, and I see cases like this all the time. . . ."). So, just to be safe, I treated myself and my bed for everything from scabies to lice. I sprayed my mattress with Lysol and Spider Killer, I washed my floor in hot water, and took my rugs to the cleaners. I even dragged my mattress—which happens to be a futon—up to the roof of my building to try and freeze anything that might be inside. All to no avail, and I still was clueless as to what it could be. I was getting about three to four hours of sleep a night at this point, and I thought I might be going crazy. All I knew was that I didn't get bitten when I went away for the weekend, or slept elsewhere. To make a long story short, I finally found a miniscule bug in my bed one night. I took it the next day in a large Tupperware container to an exterminator in New York City claiming to have "museum entomologist on staff." The lady there disappointed me gravely by telling me she wasn't an entomologist, but a professional exterminator, and as good as an entomologist. I handed over the bug. She just squinted at it and said it definitely wasn't a bed bug—too small—but that she'd look at it under a magnifying glass later. She didn't call me, and when I finally got in touch with her, she said she hadn't known what it was. When I asked her to send it back, she said she'd thrown it out. I almost cried, as it was my only proof that a bug had ever been in my bed.*

Luckily, a few nights later I found another, much larger bug. It resembled the smaller one, except that it was about seven times as large! I contained it, and saved it for when my building's exterminator would make his bi-annual (at least it feels that way) trip over, which happened to be coming in only a couple of days. He took the bug away yesterday, and I just got word that it's a bed bug. I feel horrified that that's what's been biting me, but on the other hand slightly relieved to finally know that I'm not imagining things. But now I'm worried—why didn't I ever see others? I mean, I searched all the time, everywhere, day and night. I'd turn on my light and try to surprise them. Also, a bug as large as the second one I found couldn't have been living in my futon, as there's a futon cover on it, zipped all around with no holes. And would bed bugs like living in a futon anyway? Don't they only like box springs? My futon is jammed tight with cotton, foam, and polyester fill. Should I throw it away or do you think the bugs could solely be living in the floor or somewhere. I have no wallpaper, and so far haven't found anything behind the pictures on my walls. What should I do? Where did these come from?

I'm neurotically clean, I haven't brought in any old furniture, and I've had my futon for years! (In fact, I made it when I briefly worked in a futon store, and that's why I'm really not too keen on throwing it away.)

Well, I'm sorry to be bothering you with this—you probably get a lot of strange emails from people like me. Or maybe you don't. Anyway, anyone who feeds bed bugs off the backs of their hands at seminars must be an expert. Please advise if you find you have a moment . . .

I gave Katy a bio on bed bugs and my suggested methods of treatment. There are many more emails between Katy and me over the next year or so about all of her bug problems. They would take up far too much room to include them in this book. However, I do have the complete "Katy Chronicles" on my Web page *(www.askthebugman.com)* if you are interested in reading them.

Snake Stories

I used to be into snakes many years ago and often kept them around the house. When I kept large numbers of snakes in my house, I kept frozen mice in freezer bags in the freezer. We also kept other foods in there, particularly frozen chili. One day when my ex-wife was packing her lunch for work, she reached into the freezer and grabbed a bag of what she thought was chilies. She couldn't see the contents clearly as the bag was frosted over. At work, she put her sandwich in the microwave and, while talking to someone, dumped the bag of "chilies" on her sandwich and turned on the microwave. Imagine her surprise when she opened the microwave and found her sandwich covered in cooked mice!

My ex-wife was very patient with me about snakes; she actually liked them and frequently handled them. One time she was holding a small garter snake when the doorbell rang. She didn't bother to put the snake back in its cage but just slipped it in her shirt. Unfortunately she wasn't wearing a bra at the time and the snake apparently got agitated and bit her on her nipple just as she opened the door. She ripped off her shirt in front of me, the Jehovah Witness at the door, and the whole world as she had the snake "attached" to her. The Jehovah Witness ran down the sidewalk dropping her tracts on the porch.

On another occasion my wife had to go to the restroom one night and didn't turn the light on. When she sat down she noticed there was a snake coiled around the base of the commode. Not knowing whether it was venomous she was afraid to move. She started yelling for me, but in those days I drank adult beverages and was sound asleep. She sat there all night, as the snake was sound asleep also. Finally, when I woke and went to the bathroom I saw her sitting with the king snake still in place. She couldn't move her legs from sitting there all night.

The Shopping Center Incident

Although structural fumigation is never necessary for rodent control, there was a time when we used cyanide gas (A-Dust) for rat control in Florida. We would insert a tube into a rat's burrow and pump in the cyanide. I remember a time close to thirty years ago in Florida when I got a call about rats living under a supermarket. At that time I didn't realize that rats often have two entrances to their burrows. We went to the supermarket and found about twenty rat burrows along the back of the store. We proceeded to fumigate each burrow with cyanide and plug them up. We were then standing around the truck complimenting each other on a job well done when we heard the screams. We ran around to the front of the store and witnessed something I will never forget. Women were running through the parking lot pushing shopping carts, men were standing on the top of cars screaming and children were clapping and laughing with glee. Rats were running around everywhere, as we didn't realize they had entrances to their burrows under the front of the store as well. When we heard the sirens, we quickly left so I don't know how the situation played out.

Pest Control Fiasco

A number of years ago I was a branch manager for a large pest control company located in Houston, Texas. One night a couple of my technicians went to Sugarland to treat a restaurant for German cockroaches. They arrived at the restaurant after it closed sometime around midnight. This job probably should have taken about an hour to an hour and a half.

During their rounds, the police observed my technicians' vehicle in the parking lot and then drove off. They came back two hours later and saw the vehicle and didn't think anything of it. When they made their third pass around four in the morning, the company vehicle was still in the parking lot. Getting a little suspicious, as the store lights were on, the officers entered the building through a door that the technicians didn't lock behind them. The police smelled the distinct odor of marijuana and heard laughter. They then came upon my two technicians who were in the process of killing German roaches one at a time, while smoking a joint and laughing out loud.

Needless to say my two technicians were arrested, jailed,

and fired from their job (by me). In those days the Texas legal system took a very dim view of marijuana possession, and each of those fellows pulled a five-year stint in prison.

How Not to Kill a Cockroach

I have been told this story is authentic, but I have also been told it is an urban legend. In either case, it is entertaining.

The story begins when a housewife is trying to kill a cockroach by spraying it with an entire aerosol can of insecticide. After spraying the bug and stomping on it, she put it in the toilet. When her husband returned home and had to use the bathroom, he threw a lit cigarette butt in the toilet bowl, igniting the insecticide vapors, and seriously burning his private parts. Paramedics, convulsing with laughter when carrying him on the stretcher, dropped him down the stairs, resulting in his broken pelvis and ribs.

Who said smoking isn't hazardous to your health?

13

Some Thoughts
on the Environment

❧ **In this chapter I ask Johnna about her thoughts on the use of hemp. Although this is not a "bug question," it is very important because hemp has almost no pests, while plants such as cotton have many pests and require the application of a lot of pesticides. As a matter of fact, almost half the chemicals used in agriculture are used on cotton.**

Q *In the past we have discussed the use of hemp as a crop, and our opposition to hemp being outlawed for reasons that are illogical and even vacuous. Please tell the readers why you think hemp is a valuable tool that we can use.*

A Cotton growing is probably the largest polluter on the planet in terms of releasing pesticides into the environment. The chemicals get into the soil and ground water, and poisons not only the target insects but nontarget organisms as well, including humans. Hemp, on the other hand, has long been considered a weed, but it does not require pesticides to grow. Unfortunately, it is now illegal to grow hemp in most states because of ill-informed politicians making ill-advised laws.

Hemp seed is more nutritious than soybeans, contains more essential fatty acids than any other source, and is second only to soybeans in complete protein. Further, hemp seed is high in B vitamins, is 35 percent dietary fiber, and does not contain THC. The bark of the hemp plant contains fibers that are among the world's longest soft fibers, which are also rich in cellulose. Hemp fiber is longer, more absorbent, and more insulative than cotton fiber.

According to the U.S. Department of Energy, hemp as a biomass fuel producer requires the least specialized growing and processing of all plant products. The hydrocarbons in hemp can be processed into a wide range of biomass energy sources, from fuel pellets to liquid fuels and gas. Obviously, development of biofuels could significantly reduce our consumption of fossil fuels and nuclear power.

Hemp also produces more pulp per acre than timber on a sustainable basis, and can be used in making every quality of paper. Moreover, hemp paper manufacturing could reduce wastewater contamination.

It is also interesting to note that many tobacco farmers are now looking for an alternative crop to grow. Hemp would be the perfect choice, if we can get past the rules outlawing it. During World War II, the federal government actually subsidized hemp production and farmers grew about a million acres of the plant at that time. Presidents Washington and Jefferson both grew hemp on their plantations.

Some may disagree, but I think hemp could actually save our planet. Its expanded use could mean we would not have to worry about so many pesticides and the enormous number of trees we kill to produce paper. It is apparently forgotten that all herbs, including hemp, have their uses and that we were given all of the means we need on this Earth to live a good, healthy life.

Johnna Lachnit

14

Resources and
Information

🐛 **Appearing below is information on books, suppliers, and organizations that will be helpful in maintaining a pest-free, nontoxic home or workplace.**

Books

The most helpful book you can use is *Common-Sense Pest Control* by William Olkowski, Sheila Daar, and Helga Olkowski (Newtown, Conn.: Taunton Press, 1991). This book is very helpful on identification and control of many pests. I keep a copy on my desk. Other useful books include:

> *Rodale's Garden Insect, Disease & Weed Identification Guide* by Miranda Smith and Anna Carr (Emmaus, Penn.: Rodale Press, 1988)
> *Urban Entomology: Insect and Mite Pests in the Human Environment* by William H. Robinson (London and New York: Chapman & Hall, 1996)

Suppliers

The following suppliers of equipment, least-toxic chemicals, and other materials mentioned in the book are all reputable companies that I have dealt with.

> Bug-Aside—1-866-520-5050, *www.callbugaside.com*
> This organization specializes in nontoxic pest
> control products. If they don't have what you

need, they will get if for you. They have been
very honest and ethical in their dealings with
the public.
BioQuip Products—1-310–324–0620,
   www.bioquip.com
BioQuip has a very large inventory of entomological products and entomological books. I shop
   there regularly.

Organizations

I support the following environmental organizations, and I
urge everyone to take a close look at them and then consider
supporting one or more.

The Nature Conservancy—*www.tnc.org*
The Sierra Club—*www.sierraclub.org*
Public Interest Research Group (PIRG)—
   www.pirg.org
People for the Ethical Treatment of Animals
   (PETA)—*www.peta-online.org*
Beyond Pesticides/National Coalition Against the
   Misuse of Pesticides (NCAMP)—*www.ncamp.org*

Index